ROTH IRA
for Beginners

The Ultimate Guide to Investing, Conversions, Early Retirement Hacks, Withdrawals, and Inheritance

Master Basic Skills for Growing Wealth & Retirement Planning with

Daniel Hardt

CONTENTS

Introduction

Saving up for your future might seem like a daunting task. When it comes to retirement accounts, there are so many options. Don't feel overwhelmed! With the help of this book, you will learn about how convenient and efficient it is to set yourself up for a happy and financially comfortable future. By opening a Roth IRA (Individual Retirement Account), you will be able to build a nest egg for your retirement that will not only be safely waiting for you but will also have great potential to grow into even more wealth.

A Roth IRA is an account that you can open individually, no employer help necessary. Many enjoy opening this type of account because it puts them in complete control of what they do with their money and how they invest it. The process is simple—open an account, make a contribution, and watch your wealth increase! With any financial decision, you need to be sure you understand all of the rules, deadlines, and potential penalties that come with it. This is the purpose of the book, to guide you every step of the way.

It's suggested that you begin saving for retirement as early as you can, but that doesn't mean it's too late if you haven't already.

Almost anyone can open a Roth IRA, which is why it's one of the most popular retirement savings accounts today. Based on the income that you make, you will qualify for the account and then you will be informed of what the maximum contribution you can make toward it will be. Of course, the ultimate goal is to max out your contribution so you can max out your savings. You must be realistic, so if this doesn't happen in the first year, don't fret! It's something to keep in mind and to work toward.

As you read through this book, you'll get to know all of the basics necessary before you decide to open a Roth IRA for yourself. The more you understand how it operates, the more confident you will feel about saving and investing your money. Unlike a standard savings account that holds your money until you withdraw it, a Roth IRA can do this and so much more. The interest rates are higher with this type of account, so this means if you do keep the money in there without investing, it is still going to be growing faster than it would in your normal savings account.

In addition, you have the ability to invest your contributions into stocks, bonds, mutual funds, and more. If this all sounds complex to you, it doesn't have to be! By breaking down how each of these investment opportunities works, you'll see that investing is not as complex as you once thought. Not to mention, you can contact a financial advisor who will be on your side to help you with these big financial decisions.

Moving along in the book, you will be able to read real-life examples of others who have opened Roth IRAs and how they've benefitted from the decision. When you can take an example and apply it to your own life, you'll be able to determine if opening an account is going to be a lucrative decision. As mentioned, there are many retirement accounts out there—some individually-opened and others monitored by your place of employment. Not only will this book give you a run-down of exactly what a Roth IRA is and its benefits, but it will also briefly explain some pros and cons of the other types of accounts available.

Once you decide that the Roth IRA is right for you, there is a whole chapter dedicated to investing and how to do it. You will get to read many different methods and strategies so that you're still in control of every decision you make with your money. Having a Roth IRA promises a lot of freedom with what you get to do with these funds and when you can withdraw them. Unlike some accounts that force you to wait until you've reached retirement age, you can actually withdraw your contributions at any time without penalty. This is why some use their Roth IRAs as emergency funds—you never know when unforeseen circumstances may occur, and those can be costly.

Having a Roth IRA will give you the peace of mind that you crave because you will always know exactly what is going on with your money. If you want to make a different decision, you're able to do this without the hassle and without having to go through a team of people that want to persuade you to do things differently. A Roth IRA is suitable for everyone, ranging from someone young who is just beginning to save up for their retirement to someone who is already in a later stage of life that wants an extra cushion to fall back on. Because almost everyone is eligible, there is a lot that you can do with the account depending on what your end goal is.

The aim is to give you the clearest understanding possible. Once you get through this book, all of your questions will be answered, and you can always return if you need to reference any of the information provided. Much like anything else, knowledge is power—the more you know about how a Roth IRA operates, the better you'll be able to come up with strategies that grow your money to its fullest potential. Once you see the numbers increasing, you will feel a mixed sense of relief and joy knowing that your future will be taken care of. If you're ready to learn more, read on! There are many valuable topics to cover, and it all begins right now.

1

INTRODUCTION TO ROTH IRA

You've been told countless times—it's never too early to start saving for your future. Thinking about opening a retirement account, even when you are well into your adult years, can seem taxing and overwhelming. What does it all mean? Now is your chance to fully understand the topic so you can set yourself up for a financially healthy future. A Roth IRA is represented by an acronym—Individual Retirement Account. So, how does this fit into your life and what are the benefits of having one? Most people assume that they can simply store money away into their regular savings accounts, but it becomes easy to make withdrawals whenever you want to buy a new gadget or get a fantastic birthday present for a friend. Saving money can be tough! This is why the Roth IRA can set you up on a better financial path.

What Is a Roth IRA?

Starting with the very basics, your first goal is to understand this type of account. This is going to give you a foundational understanding of how to successfully save money. In the simplest terms, a Roth IRA is like a savings account in which you can invest your hard-earned money. Its glamour comes from two huge benefits:

1. Your wealth grows tax-free over time.

2. You can withdraw tax-free when you retire.

The tax advantages play a large part in why it's the favorite child of retirement accounts. It shouldn't be confused with its cousin, the traditional IRA, which sounds similar but is fundamentally different.

The main distinction between a Roth IRA and a traditional IRA is how they're taxed. With a Roth IRA, your account is funded with after-tax dollars, meaning that you won't have to pay any taxes on your money once you start to withdraw it. These funds can come from income that you earn or even gifted money. Another important factor to consider is that the contributions you put in are not tax-deductible, meaning that your Roth IRA contributions will not lower your taxable income. If you were to open a traditional IRA, the money you put into the account would be deducted from your taxes, but you would then have to pay income tax on it if you decided to withdraw any funds at the current income tax rate.

For most people who are just starting out with retirement accounts, the Roth IRA is going to be the better option because you won't be met with any surprise tax payments if you do end up needing the funds. It's a very transparent type of account which typically makes the Roth IRA a great choice. Something to consider is that as people age, they generally move higher in tax brackets as they advance their careers over time. This means you're likely to be in a higher tax bracket once you reach retirement age. Luckily for you, your higher tax bracket at retirement age won't affect you as much because you've contributed with after-tax dollars!

Take Emily as an example, she was a 21-year-old student who decided to open a Roth IRA account after taking the advice from her parents. At the time, she didn't understand what the big deal was between the Roth IRA and the traditional. She thought that they were both almost identical, which they are if you do not consider the taxes you might have to pay once you need to start withdrawing your money. Now 65, Emily is thankful that she went with the Roth IRA option all those years ago because she's in a tax bracket that is several ranks above the one she was in when she was a 21-year-old student. If she had gone with the traditional IRA, each withdrawal after retirement would be taxed at the rate of the highest tax bracket she's ever been in.

Retirement Plans for Beginners

Roth IRAs are also great for people who are just starting out with their retirement plans because it is likely they qualify. To put money into your Roth IRA account, you need to look into the contribution limits for the given year. In the year 2021, you can only contribute to a Roth IRA if you make $140,000 or below (Segal, 2020). You likely fall into this category, which is great. This means that a Roth IRA would be compatible with your savings plan! If you are married, this limit changes—if you make $208,000 as a couple or below, you can each contribute to a Roth IRA account.

The actual amount of money that you can put into your Roth IRA also varies. In 2021, the contribution limit is $6,000 yearly, unless you are older than 50 (Segal, 2020). If you are older than 50, this amount gets bumped up to $7,000. Considering the example with Emily, the 21-year-old student, it's unlikely that she would be able to contribute the full $6,000 to her account in a year, which is perfectly okay. Some people are only able to put in $50, $100, and so on, but this is still better than having nothing tucked away for the future. Eventually, your end goal is likely to be able to max out on your contribution each year.

Almost any bank that you use can offer you a Roth IRA, and they can talk to you more about the details of opening one if you schedule an appointment with a financial advisor. At this appointment, you will likely discuss your current income level, how much you want to save over the years, and how much you will be able to contribute. It's also important to keep in mind how much you think you will be withdrawing from the account before you reach retirement age. Life is unpredictable, and anything can happen—you might need to access your funds sooner than expected in case of an emergency or a tight financial situation. Knowing that you have this account in place can give you a serious confidence boost, especially during hard financial times like the ones that many have been experiencing lately.

What Are the Benefits of Having a Roth IRA?

Now that you have an idea of what a Roth IRA is, picture it in your current financial situation. How can it help you? This is important because your hard-earned money should be kept safe. Let's look over some of the benefits of having a Roth IRA account. They might resonate with you and your current situation:

1. **The Tax Break Benefit**: Because you are putting money into your account that you've earned and that has already been taxed, you do not have to pay additional taxes on it when you must make a withdrawal. It's important to think about tax season, even if it seems far away. Depending on which tax bracket you fall into for the year, you might end up owing money instead of receiving a refund—this can be an annoying and inconvenient realization to come across on April 15th when you were not thinking about it prior.

2. **Monetary Growth**: When your money is in a Roth IRA account, it has the potential to grow exponentially through your investments—that's right! Over the course of a year, your Roth IRA could grow hundreds of dollars in your sleep, whereas a traditional savings account may only earn you a few dollars. You are probably familiar with earning interest with a traditional savings account, but this percentage rate is typically so low that you only end up with a few extra cents at the end of each year. Your Roth IRA has a better chance of helping your money grow tax-free through interest payments, dividends, and capital gains. The best part is that your money works for you while you sit back and relax! In a later chapter, you are going to learn about exactly what you must do if you want to make your money grow. Investing is not a hard or complicated topic that can only be understood by those who grind on Wall Street each week— you are able to do the same thing with your own money in your Roth IRA account.

3. **Investment Flexibility**: Once you open a Roth IRA account, you can invest your money however you want. This is a great benefit because the typical 401(k) plan that some employers provide usually comes with limits. They will tell you where and how you can invest, which will definitely limit your monetary growth in the long-run. Having flexibility is important because it means you can customize your investment portfolio to what suits you and your circumstances the best. As mentioned, in a later chapter, you will learn about all of the different ways you can invest your money and what it means to actually do so.

There are several different investment accounts that you can open, but this book focuses on the Roth IRA because it has huge tax advantages that many people can benefit from. It's no wonder it's grown to be a crowd favorite. Once you have an understanding of how to open one and what to do with it once you have one, you will see that there isn't anything too complicated about the process. Plus, you can always discuss your options with the financial advisor at your bank who helped you open the account if you are unsure.

Can a Roth IRA Help to Increase Your Wealth?

Yes, it can! One of the main financial goals that people strive for is to increase their wealth after opening a Roth IRA. A large factor in growing wealth is contributing your earned income consistently and allowing it time to grow. Contributing earned income benefits you because, unlike some retirement accounts, you aren't relying on borrowed money to create your financial foundation. Since there is no minimum contribution required, you can simply take $20 from each paycheck that you receive and put it into your Roth IRA account. It might seem insignificant at the time, but this money will add up through earnings on your investments and compound interest.

Once this money is in your account, there are plenty of exciting possibilities in terms of what you can do with it. Eduardo initially had no idea that his money could be invested into stocks, bonds, CDs, and money market funds when he was making his $20 weekly contributions. This growth potential kept him motivated to keep adding funds to the account, even if it was tempting to take that extra money and use it for recreational expenses. Once you realize the full potential of the Roth IRA, you will start to feel excited about saving money and investing because you'll understand the power of a single dollar.

You can see that there is a big difference between a Roth IRA and the standard savings account that you've probably been using for years. While there's nothing wrong with having an easy-access savings account, it's also tempting. It's a good idea to spread your money around into accounts separate from your disposable spending income in order to create more growth potential. Make a plan for yourself that involves putting money into your Roth IRA, investing it, and allowing it to grow. The less you are tempted to withdraw from this account, the more that it will grow before your eyes. Eduardo was pleasantly surprised to see his investment grow a few hundred dollars after only a few months of contributing to his Roth IRA. In just a few months, he gained more than his standard savings account would've grown in 20 years. Note, however, that the money in your account will fluctuate with the market, but it always exponentially increases in wealth over the years.

Imagine how great it will feel knowing that you have money that is being invested and that it can grow while you sleep—you don't need to do anything else except monitor the funds! This can provide you with a huge feeling of peace of mind, especially during today's uncertain financial circumstances. It's never too early or too late to start planning for your future.

Can You Use a Roth IRA for Early Retirement?

You can absolutely use your Roth IRA to help set you up for early retirement—this takes strategy and discipline. It can be very difficult to convince yourself to put money away for an unknown date in the future when there are many things that you'd like to buy presently. Some people are better than others when it comes to saving money—this is true—but it is a muscle that can be strengthened. It's always important to think about the bigger picture and how seemingly insignificant spending can impact whether or not you achieve your long-term goals. You need to ask yourself what is more worthwhile and valuable to you. Do you really need to buy that new car that depreciates in value the moment it leaves the lot? Or do you want to put that money into your Roth IRA so that your money can appreciate and grow into a reservoir of wealth to put towards your dream life?

With any type of money-saving strategy you imagine, there is a sense of sacrifice that must be made. You need to truly think about your priorities and decide what is most important to you. Carla was faced with a tough decision as she was about to turn 30— she lived in a good neighborhood in her parents' older home. It was a great spot for her and her family to live, but she always envied her friends who seemed to be moving up the ladder while she remained in the same spot. In response, Carla gravitated toward the brand new homes in high-class neighborhoods as she contemplated spending her hard-earned savings on what she believed would make herself feel competent.

Even though she lived rent-free in a beautiful paid-off home, it turns out she was just envious of her friends who seemingly had it all. Realizing this, she made the decision to put aside her pride and put her money into her Roth IRA instead of creating stress for herself in the form of debt. She allowed the money in her Roth IRA to grow for her, and because of this, she was able to retire earlier than any of her friends. She made a sacrifice that seemed difficult at the moment, but it greatly benefited her in the future.

Now that Carla is young and retired, she has a lot of time to plan out exactly where she wants to live and what kind of house she is searching for. Also, because she did not make a rash decision in the past, she is able to watch the housing market to ensure that she is making the purchase at the best time possible. Though she sacrificed something while she was in her 30s, she is now able to feel like she has the redemption that she deserves at the young age of 45. It's all about perspective and thinking about the options that you have available to you right now. This is why it's never too late or too early to begin investing your money.

As you read through all of the options that are available with the Roth IRA, it's important to remember that everyone is in a different financial state right now. Do not feel bad if you can't contribute thousands to your account each year but know that any contribution is going to serve as a positive safety net for your future. This book is meant to be used as a reference for you to gain knowledge about the account and if it fits into your life right now. While it might not be possible to open your own Roth IRA at the moment, you will be well-equipped with all of the information that you need to potentially open one in the future.

There are many people who choose to open Roth IRAs well into their adult years, and this is not due to laziness or an inability to make the decision. One of the biggest things that stop people from opening these accounts is that they feel that they are not qualified. One of the myths that surround the Roth IRA is that you need to contribute large sums of money to get started, but each account varies. If you contact your local bank, having a meeting with a financial advisor can be very beneficial in your decision-making process. They will be able to walk you through each step necessary to open a Roth IRA and what the recommended contribution amount is.

A lot of people are also unsure about having to pay taxes on this money once they decide to withdraw. As you've learned, one of the biggest benefits of having a Roth IRA is that the money you contribute is placed in the account post-taxed, meaning you won't have to worry about paying taxes on it at the end. It's truly a win-win situation for you if you want to get started in the investing world. Almost anyone can open an account, and it's worthwhile to see what your options are.

2

IS A ROTH IRA RIGHT FOR YOU?

Most individuals are eligible to open a Roth IRA account, but there are some factors to consider that depend on your tax filing status and modified adjusted gross income (MAGI). It's important that you are aware of potential limitations on your eligibility and whether or not they apply to you:

- Filing an individual tax return or joint tax return through marriage affects your contribution limits.
- Depending on the year you're contributing, you must not make over a certain amount of money or else you will not be able to make a full contribution to your Roth IRA.

However, if you do make too much money by Roth IRA standards, don't worry. Later, we'll be discussing how you can utilize the backdoor Roth method to contribute the max amount regardless of your high income.

To get a better idea of what this all means for you, the following information from 2020 and 2021 should help (Lake, 2020):

Category	Income Range for 2020 Contributions	Income Range for 2021 Contribution
Married, filing a joint tax return.	**Full:** Less than $196,000 **Partial:** $196,000 to $205,999 **Not eligible:** $206,000	**Full:** Less than $198,000 **Partial:** From $198,000 to $207,000 **Not eligible:** more than $208,000
Married, filing separate tax returns, lived together with spouse at any point in the year.	**Partial:** Less than $10,000 **Not eligible:** Greater than or equal to $10,000	**Partial:** Less than $10,000 **Not eligible:** Greater than or equal to $10,000
Single, head of household, or married and filing a separate tax return. Did not live with a spouse at any point in the year.	**Full:** Less than $124,000 **Partial:** $124,000 to $138,999 **Not eligible:** Greater than or equal to $139,000	**Full:** Less than $125,000 **Partial:** From $125,000 to $139,999 **Not eligible:** Greater than or equal to $140,000

Your income level can change depending on the job or position you hold. This is why some people might be eligible to make contributions one year but be unable to the next. When an individual contributes to their Roth IRA account, this means that they fall into one of the above income categories. However, if you do make too much money to contribute, there are legal loopholes that allow you to make full contributions that we will discuss later.

For the Spousal Roth IRA, things work a little differently. If the couple wants to boost their contributions, one person can fund the account on behalf of their partner. In order to make a contribution on behalf of their spouse, the following must be taken into consideration:

1. The couple must be married and file a joint tax return.
2. The individual who is making the contribution must have eligible compensation.
3. The total contribution for each individual must not exceed the taxable income reported at the end of the year.

Roth IRAs can't be joint accounts, so each individual must have their own. This is when the Spousal Roth IRA rules come into play and how a couple can still grow their wealth, even when one partner makes less money than the other.

Pros and Cons

Let's weigh out the pros and cons of different retirement accounts to give you a clear idea of your options. The retirement accounts being compared are Employer Traditional 401(k), Employer Roth 401(k), Non-Employer Individual Traditional IRA, and Non-Employer Individual Roth IRA. This list is not exhaustive of all types of retirement accounts, however, they are very common. Understanding which one to choose can change a lot about the way that you save money in the future.

Employer Traditional 401(k)

Pros:

• Your employer will withhold the pre-tax dollars for you from each paycheck and contribute it to your 401(k) plan, so you do not have to be responsible for moving the money around.

• When you start your plan, you get to choose the percentage of your paycheck that goes toward your 401(k) plan.

• In some workplaces, your employer might match your contribution.

• If you have a balance of less than $1,000, your employer can write you a check for the amount. This is a plus because you get the money in-hand. You can use it immediately after you deposit the check.

• If you have a balance of at least $5,000, your employer can't remove your money from the 401(k) plan unless you give them permission. This gives you more financial control of your retirement plan. It prevents any unwanted changes without your permission.

Cons:

• Under certain circumstances, your employer can remove funds from your account after you leave the company.

• If your balance is between $1,000-$5,000, your employer reserves the right to move your funds between different IRA accounts.

• The $5,000 rule above in the pros only applies to funds that you contributed from the earnings you made at the given job. If you change jobs, this might no longer apply.

• Employers are not required to offer you a 401(k) plan.

• Your money has the potential to grow tax-deferred, but you will have to pay taxes on it once you decide to retire (you must make a withdrawal of a certain amount each year).

Employer Roth 401(k)

Pros:

• Since your contributions are tax-deductible, you won't have to claim this money as earnings when you file your taxes—very beneficial for those in high tax brackets.

• If you are at least 59 1/2 years old and have been contributing to your plan for at least five years, you qualify for tax-free withdrawals.

• If you need to make withdrawals before then, there are ways to still do this tax-free when it comes to a case of disability.

• Regardless of how much money you make, you can still contribute to your employer's Roth 401(k) plan up to the yearly contribution limit.

• The limits are $19,500 if you are under 50 and $26,000 if you are older than 50—much more than the standard Roth IRA account allows.

Cons:

• If you have both an employer Roth IRA account and an individual Roth IRA account, the contribution limit applies to both of them together, not individually.

• There are harsh penalties that you will face if you do not make a withdrawal from your account by the time you reach 70 ½.

Non-Employer Individual Traditional IRA

Pros:

- Taxes are not taken out of your contributions, meaning that your taxable income is minimized.
- If you are already in a high tax bracket, this can work to your advantage because it won't add more to your taxable income.
- When contributing to a Traditional IRA, the income brackets are much lower ($66,000 or less for a single head of household in 2021).
- If you are a single head of household, you can make a full deduction up to the amount you've contributed.

Cons:

- If you make between $66,000 and $76,000 in 2021, you are only able to make a partial deduction.
- If you make over $76,000, you do not qualify for any deduction.
- If you are under 59 ½, you face a 10% penalty plus any taxes owed if you withdraw any money before this point.
- There is a required withdrawal that must be made by the time you are 72—life expectancy and that year's taxable income is the formula that determines how much you must withdraw.

Non-Employer Individual Roth IRA

Pros:

- Your contributions are made with after-tax dollars, meaning no surprises when it comes to filing your income taxes.
- You get the chance to build your assets in a tax-free way when the money is in your account.

- You can make withdrawals from your account at any time, as long as the sum is equal to your contributions made.

Cons:

- The strict yearly contribution limits might hinder you if you want to invest more money.

- Since you are paying your taxes upfront; this can be either a pro or con depending on if you need that extra money throughout the year.

- You have to set the account up for yourself, which many find intimidating.

One of the main things to remember about all of the above accounts is that none of them are mutually exclusive. Just because you decide to open your own individual Roth IRA does not mean you won't also take advantage of an employee-offered account in the future. Because you have this freedom of choice, there are many possibilities when it comes to saving and growing your money. Getting rid of the misconception that your first choice is your final choice will put you at ease. Understand that you can also utilize multiple retirement accounts to support your goals.

Overall, it's typically the individual Roth IRA that gets selected because it's the most straightforward of all the IRA accounts. Though you can open multiple accounts, it's a no brainer that a Roth IRA account should be one of them. People already invested in a Roth IRA like having the ability to access their contributions at any time without penalties, and the fact that the contributions are made with after-tax dollars. Some even revolve their early retirement plans around their Roth IRA. It's a straightforward account to have, especially if you're just starting out with retirement planning and investing.

Carmen just took a job at an insurance agency that offered her an employer-provided traditional 401(k) plan. This was very exciting, as none of her previous jobs had ever offered the same. Before she agreed to sign off on any paperwork, she was feeling confused about all of the terms and conditions. Upon doing some more research and speaking with her local banker, she realized that she felt more comfortable investing her money into an individual Roth IRA account. She did not know if this account would be the one that she planned on keeping her entire retirement savings in, and she also did not know how long she planned to stay at her new insurance job. Because she realized that a lot could change on short notice, she opted to open her own account and decline her employer-provided 401(k) plan.

There are many people who are faced with similar problems as the one Carmen was faced with. Investing your money can seem very complicated at first glance but breaking each account down into pros and cons can help tremendously. Seeing everything on paper gives you the chance to think about what you would truly like to do with your hard-earned income. It also encourages you to not only think about the present but the future, too. Something that might sound fantastic at the moment might not be the best decision for yourself in the long-term.

There is nothing wrong with admitting that you do not understand a plan or if you have additional questions about it—nobody knows what they are doing at first, which is why questions help you to learn! Never sign off on any paperwork that you do not feel fully committed to, especially when it comes to bank accounts. With the help of this book, the Roth IRA is explained in simple terms to allow you the chance to fully comprehend exactly what it is and why it can benefit you. There is no need to guess which one you should open or to blindly select one because you feel pressured into it. Take your time, and do your research.

Real-Life Examples

When choosing a retirement account, it helps to hear about stories that other people have gone through because you will be better able to relate to them. Reading about technical terms and limitations gets confusing and boring. In the following example, you will learn about the issues that you might face if you decide to open a traditional IRA account and a Roth IRA account. The main thing to remember is that the contribution limit applies to the accounts simultaneously, not individually. Being aware of how much you can contribute each year is important, which is why the chart above was created so you can reference which category you fall into.

Adina's Decision

Adina turned 26, and she knew that she had to start saving up for her future. Her parents had always warned her that she needed something to fall back on in case her dream of becoming a freelance artist did not work out in the end. Being a freelancer, Adina never had a steady paycheck to rely on. Some weeks were great for her, landing jobs that paid her rent and bills for the entire month. Then, there were some weeks where she had no money at all. Without any money and without any savings to fall back on, Adina realized that her parents were entirely right—something had to change.

This is when she walked into her local bank to talk about if opening an IRA account was smart for her given situation. After some discussion, she decided to go with the Roth IRA. It was straightforward, and she liked the idea of being able to make withdrawals whenever necessary due to her income instability. She kept this account open for a few years, making small contributions when she had her good weeks. Eventually, she was able to save up around $3,000, which made her very proud of herself.

Being older now, Adina felt much more comfortable in her ability to save money. She ended up landing a job that paid her a salary, so she decided to visit her local bank again to discuss what other accounts she qualified for. She decided to open a traditional IRA account, but she did not think to ask as many questions this time because she was already very familiar with her Roth IRA. In her mind, she was going to be able to make double the contributions and make double the wealth. It turns out that she did not realize the yearly contribution amount applied to both accounts together. She was only able to invest about half as much as she thought she would in her traditional IRA that year.

Seeing this as a lesson learned, Adina still decided to keep both accounts because they serve unique purposes. She placed more of her money into her Roth IRA since the contributions were after-tax dollars, and she used her traditional IRA as an account she viewed she would never touch until she was fully ready to retire. Being able to withdraw money occasionally from her Roth IRA, she was able to create a sustainable savings plan for herself within only a few years. She did feel guilty for starting the process so late, but she realized that it was better late than never.

Maxing Out

Jonathan decided to open his Roth IRA account when he was 19 years old. He was moving from his hometown to an apartment of his own a few hours away, so he knew that he needed to set himself up with a hefty savings account that could grow with him. After securing a job in marketing, he felt that he had it made. The salary that he was earning allowed him to quickly make the maximum contribution to his Roth IRA account within his first year of having it—a very proud accomplishment for him. While he was able to do this, he was still left with a burning question—what to do with the remainder of the money that he was still able to save.

Understandably, this is not a situation that most people are faced with. Having an abundance of money in these times is a rarity, but for Jonathan, it became his reality. He did not want to simply put the rest of his money into a low-interest savings account because he still wanted it to grow, but he also did not want to open a traditional IRA account because of the taxes he would have to pay at the end. Unfortunately, his marketing job did not offer any sort of 401(k) plans—he felt stuck.

Eventually, Jonathan got married, so he was able to make contributions to his wife's Roth IRA account. This solved his dilemma, and he realized that his own account was growing remarkably because of his investment choices. When you put your money into a Roth IRA account, it's not simply sitting there and gaining interest. You have investment opportunities by way of stocks and bonds. With the help of his financial advisor, Jonathan was able to pick out some stocks that he decided to invest in. By the time the next year came around, he realized that he had nearly doubled his maximum contribution! This was not only a fantastic milestone for him but for his wife, as well. It turns out that they were expecting a baby the following year.

Of course, the ultimate goal should be to max out your contribution amount every single year that you can. While it's not possible for everyone, it's definitely something to strive for. Your money can grow very quickly without you having to do anything in return. In Jonathan's case, quickly maxing out his account meant that he now had a secure future to provide to his future child and growing family. Later in the book, we will discuss even more benefits to maxing out your account contributions and why you should do it.

Saving without Investing

Francesca had been wanting to open a Roth IRA account for herself for a few years, but she just hadn't gotten around to it. Finally, after a temporary shift in her job situation, she decided that it was time to secure an account for herself. Realizing that she didn't have much in savings as her workplace cut her hours made her see how necessary it was to open a Roth IRA for her future. Going into the bank, Francesca didn't really know much about the account at all. Investing was something that she was entirely unfamiliar with.

After the banker explained to her that she had several options to invest in, Francesca still wasn't quite sold on the whole process. She realized that there was a slight risk that came along with investing her money instead of letting it grow at a high interest rate. At the end of her meeting, she ultimately decided to just make a contribution without making any investments. Not only is this okay to do, but many others feel the same way. You can't expect yourself to feel comfortable with investing your hard-earned money into stocks, bonds, or CDs that you are still unsure of.

Francesca allowed a few months to go by to see how she was feeling about the money in her Roth IRA account. She could see that her interest rate was still working to her advantage, and she felt that was good enough for the contributions that she was making on a regular basis once her job schedule picked back up. Throughout Francesca's entire time of having her Roth IRA account, she did not ever choose to invest her money, but it still served as a great retirement account by the time that she was ready. This is not an uncommon option, and it's important to remember that you might not be the only one who has this mindset.

You already know that a Roth IRA differs from a traditional savings account because of the way that the contributions are made and how you get to withdraw them, so there is a difference between the two. Even if you simply want your money to sit in your Roth IRA account untouched for decades, you can choose to do this because it's a very personal choice. Until you reach an age where you must make your withdrawal, you do not have to even touch the account again, which can give you a nice feeling of peace of mind. Sometimes, having your money out of sight will keep you motivated to save it because it won't be so easily accessible for spending.

How to Establish Financial Goals

When you are considering opening a Roth IRA account, this comes along with two factors—the contribution of your money and your chance to invest it. How can you be certain if investing is right for you? To better assess this decision, it helps to go over your current financial goals. Think about what you are trying to do in life and where you see yourself in the next five to 10 years. How much money will you need to save to turn your dreams into a reality?

Most professionals will give you the same advice—if you are unsure about investing right now, you should at least be regularly contributing to a liquid savings account. This is a standard savings account which typically has a low interest rate and is connected to a checking account. Getting into the habit of saving money in this account can make it easier to prepare for investing in a retirement account. However, liquid accounts can be difficult to deal with because they are so easily accessible. If you want to "borrow" money from your savings account to put into your checking account, you can typically do this with the click of a button. It takes a lot of self-control to keep your money in the right account.

This is not to say that your liquid emergency savings account is useless—it's actually the opposite. Having both an accessible savings account and a Roth IRA is a great way to get on the path to better financial stability. Once you are ready, schedule a meeting with your local banker to talk about your Roth IRA options and if you feel that you would like to invest or not.

When you have big financial goals that matter to you, this will help motivate you to save and invest. You'll have to decide what is most important to you in your life right now, and this is exactly what you must do to establish solid financial goals for yourself. Ask yourself the following questions as a guideline:

- *Are you currently on your permanent career path?*
- *Would you like to move or purchase a house in the next few years?*

- *Are you going to have a wedding in the next few years?*
- *Do you plan on starting a family?*
- *Are there any trips that you've been saving up for?*
- *Do you anticipate that you will start or resume any hobbies?*
- *Do you want to retire early?*

By answering these questions, it should become clearer to you that you might need to save up more money than you currently have. For each of these questions, decide if they apply to you and then look up the expected cost. Maybe you'd like to purchase a house in the next five years. If you live in an area where houses cost $200,000 and want to make a 10% down payment, then you'll need to save up $20,000. You would also need to estimate your expected mortgage payments and make sure they fit your budget. Once you know how much money you'll need for each goal, you can prioritize which to pursue first and make a plan to save up for them.

Keep in mind that your financial goals won't look like anyone else's. They are going to be personally tailored to your needs and desires in life and are meant to benefit your future. Take an honest look at how you've been doing so far with your liquid savings account. If you've been struggling to save money, try starting with some smaller financial goals such as saving $20 a week in your liquid savings account. This can get you into the habit of saving money, allowing you to open a Roth IRA and commit to your contributions with confidence.

A big part of making financial goals and sticking to them is tracking where your money goes. After all, if it doesn't get measured, it doesn't get managed. By knowing how you currently spend your money, you'll have the opportunity to cut unnecessary expenses and direct that money to your savings. Meaning you can reach your goals even faster! Along the way, you'll track your savings contributions and how close you are to reaching your goal. You can also use your current budget to help calculate how much you need to save. In the house purchase example, you can compare your current rent payment to your expected mortgage payment to know in advance whether you'll need to make changes to your budget, income, or savings to afford the mortgage.

Tracking your spending and budgeting can seem intimidating at first, but they become much easier with a little practice. Just follow these steps:

• Make a spreadsheet online that you'll use to track your monthly spending.

• Each month record how much you spent in total, and then divide that into essential expenses and non-essential expenses. Essentials include things such as your mortgage or rent payment, utilities, phone bills, school loans, groceries, etc. Non-essential spending could include eating out, entertainment, shopping, and other discretionary purchases.

• Set aside the last day of the month to review your spending habits. You might be surprised by how much you spend in certain categories and be inspired to improve your money habits.

• Once you've done this consistently over the course of a year, you can review your overall spending and make a budget plan for the upcoming year. Think ahead. Write down the recurring and one-time expenses you know will come such as rent, dental procedures, birthdays, vacations, savings, and of course your Roth IRA contributions.

• Look at your take-home salary and divide it by 12 months to effectively set a monthly budget for your essential expenses, anticipated expenses, and non-essential recreational expenses. Of course, it's important to set aside money for your own enjoyment as well.

Saving money shouldn't feel like a punishment as long as you're being smart and planning ahead. If your financial situation ever changes, be sure to revisit your financial plan quarterly to adjust your numbers. Financial planning doesn't have to be stressful. Give every dollar a job, and all you have to do is enjoy the fruits of your diligence.

It's okay if you notice that you have flaws in the way you spend your money while working on your budget—you aren't the only one. Try looking at these flaws as opportunities to improve by setting and pursuing your goals. Assessing how well you can save money right now will also let you know how much you should invest when you open your Roth IRA account. If you know that you are bad at saving money, work on the smaller goals mentioned above until you are confident you won't need to withdraw your contributions. Remember, you don't need to know everything in the beginning. This is why you are reading this book—the purpose is to make your life easier, not more complicated.

3

THINGS TO KNOW BEFORE STARTING

Before opening your Roth IRA account, it's essential that you take time to understand the contribution limits and how they work. Based on your age group, earned income, and the year, you are going to be met with different limits. Because this is something that does change on an annual basis, you cannot assume that what you contributed in 2020 will also apply to 2021. To get the most up-to-date information, you need to do a little research before moving forward. When it comes to any type of monetary investment, it's always important to have all of the facts before you move any of your finances around.

This chapter will break down everything you need to know about having a Roth IRA account, from how to contribute to it to the rules that apply when you must withdraw from it. Though it's a simple and easy to understand account, there are different ways that you can go about using it. All of the information is valuable because it directly impacts your future. If you decide to open your own Roth IRA account, you have the potential to increase your wealth with ease—most people don't even realize this is possible!

Full Contribution Limits

This year, the Roth IRA contribution limit is $6,000 if you are under 50 and $7,000 if you are over 50. What this means is that this was the maximum amount of money you can put into your Roth IRA account in the current contribution period, even if you have some extra money saved up. While this contribution limit can change, it is not going to change for the upcoming year, so the same limits apply. If you would like to make a full contribution—to max out your contribution—you can do so with either $6,000 or $7,000, depending on your age.

It's important to note that the Roth IRA contribution timeline does not follow the typical January through December schedule of a regular year. For example, in 2020, you have from January 1st until April 15th of 2021 to contribute to your Roth IRA—the same as the tax year. If you can remember that your Roth IRA account follows this same calendar, you should have no problem remembering to make your full contribution before it's time to file your taxes.

Don't be hard on yourself if you can't make a full contribution in your first year, or first few years, of having a Roth IRA. While maxing out is definitely a great goal to have, making as big of a contribution as you can is still going to benefit you. Think about it this way—it is money that you are setting aside for your future that you did not have set aside at the beginning of the year. When your money is in a Roth IRA account, it is not only being protected but being encouraged to grow. This is how you are able to secure such a solid foundation for yourself.

To make a contribution, you can either use earned income or money that you receive elsewhere, such as a gift from a relative. There are some instances in which there are some funds that will not be accepted as Roth IRA contributions. These are:

- Alimony
- Child support
- Income from rental property
- Interest and dividends from investments
- Pay received while inside a penal institution
- Retirement income
- Social Security benefits
- Unemployment benefits

These are not acceptable sources of income because they are not being earned. These are either benefits that you are earning because of a certain reason or because you are a part of a government program. Earned income is money that you work for and receive from an employer.

To make a full contribution to your Roth IRA account, you have to make at least the same in earned income. This means that if you only made $3,000 during the 2020 contribution period, that is the maximum amount of money you would be able to contribute to your Roth IRA account. Luckily, most who are employed will easily pass the $6,000 (or $7,000) threshold in a contribution year, but you do need to earn this much money before you are able to make the full contribution.

There are some cases where an individual might be working but might still not be able to make a full contribution because of other circumstances. Someone who is in school and only working part-time for a few months is a good example, but this does not mean that they cannot open a Roth IRA to still save for their future. Making a full contribution to the best of your ability is still a lot better than not having a safety net to fall back on.

Partial Contribution Limits

There are some cases when you're only going to be able to make a partial contribution. One example of this, aside from not earning enough income during the tax year, is if you are in a higher income bracket. For the present year, if you are an individual and make between $124,000 and $138,999 annually, then you don't get to make a full contribution. A term to familiarize yourself with is that you begin to "phase out." What this means is that you will be ineligible to contribute up to the maximum yearly amount because of how much income you make. In this case, only a partial contribution from the maximum of the $6,000 (or $7,000) that is based on your income can be made. These limits can change if you make between $125,000 to $139,000, then you will start to phase out.

Of course, nobody wants to feel that they're limited in the amount of money they can contribute to their Roth IRA account, especially if they have it in earned income. Some people work around this rule by using a method known as a "backdoor IRA." This is not an official retirement account, but it's an informal title for a method that is meant for individuals who make a higher income, around $124,000 annually. A backdoor Roth IRA can continue to fund their Roth IRA account in excess of the limit.

Sometimes, a traditional IRA account can be opened to serve as your "backdoor." This allows you to legally work around the income limits that come with Roth IRA contribution rules. What will happen is that you will turn your traditional IRA account into a Roth IRA account. This does involve filling out a tax form and being mindful of the pro-rata rule, which states that the balance of all IRAs must be zero by December 31st of the conversion year. When you do this, you can roll funds over from your traditional account into your Roth account. There are no limits to how much money you can roll over, even if it's more than the annual allowed Roth IRA contribution limit. As long as the funds are already existing in the traditional account, you should be able to do this to save up even more money.

Another way to use a traditional IRA account to your advantage is to convert it into a Roth IRA account. With the help of a financial advisor, they will be able to walk you through this process. It's not something that you can do on your own or online. The same idea can also apply to an existing 401(k) account. Each investor is able to complete one Roth IRA conversion per year, so choose wisely if you're planning on using this strategy.

This is not something that'll force you to dodge paying taxes because it is legal. Something to consider is that doing this will actually potentially increase your taxes—this is the downfall. You must weigh out your options. Would you rather pay more taxes and save more money for retirement or pay fewer taxes and save less money? The reason why your taxes could go up is that the funds that are rolled over count as earned income. If you roll over enough money, you might be boosted into a higher tax bracket.

Another factor to consider is that funds you rollover are not considered typical contributions—they are converted funds. This means that you will have to wait five years to gain access to them penalty-free if you are under 59 ½. For some, this doesn't matter because a Roth IRA account is one that won't be touched until retirement. In this case, the decision is beneficial. Those who use their Roth IRA as an emergency account should think twice about using any backdoor methods since the money can't be quickly accessed.

Exceeding Your Limit

When you have a Roth IRA account, attention to detail is necessary. Pay attention to how much you are contributing, or else you might accidentally exceed your limit. If you end up contributing more than you are supposed to, without using one of the backdoor methods mentioned earlier, you will face tax laws that can impose an additional 6% tax on the money for each year it remains in the IRA account. Surprisingly, going over the limit is easier than you'd imagine. If you don't pay close attention to how much you are contributing, you might put too much money in the account without even realizing it.

Seeking assistance from a financial professional is a wise decision when you have any type of retirement account. They are basically going to provide you with calculations and advice that you might not be aware of if you are doing this on your own. A financial advisor will also be able to help you monitor your income, which can change due to many different circumstances. You might earn a promotion or get a new job, and either of these instances can move you into a higher income bracket. Then, you'll start to phase out how much money you can contribute to your Roth IRA account.

If you find that you've accidentally contributed too much, there are steps you can take to remedy the situation a little bit.
Withdraw the Excess

If you realize you have contributed too much and you haven't filed your taxes yet, you can withdraw the excess funds to avoid paying the additional 6% in taxes for each year the money is in your Roth IRA account. You won't owe any additional federal income tax on this excess contribution if you withdraw it, but you could end up owing additional federal income tax on the earnings and an additional 10% federal tax if you are under 59 ½. Again, this all comes down to what kind of strategy you decide to use and what your current priorities are.

Carry the Excess Forward

If you have already filed your taxes and it is at least six months after Tax Day, you can carry the excess funds forward to be applied to next year's contributions. Remember that it is still possible to exceed the limit for the following year too, depending on how much excess you have. If you can calculate this carefully, this will become your way to avoid paying the annual 6% tax on the excess contributions made in the future. The downfall is that you will have to end up paying the 6% tax for the year that you exceeded your limit.

The key thing to remember is that you don't need to panic! If you do go over your contribution limit, you still have options available to lessen the penalties. For any further help with this, you can ask your financial advisor what your best approach is. Having another set of eyes on your monetary situation is always a good idea because you might be overlooking options that you have simply because you don't know about them yet.

No doubt, this process can still feel very complicated, especially if you are relatively new to managing retirement accounts. Another person that would be great to consult with is your tax advisor. You might need to fill out certain forms to provide to the IRS if you need to correct an excess contribution, so it is better to be safe than sorry.

Deadlines

With any bank account, there are important deadlines to become aware of, especially the kind that allows you to make contributions. Look at your money as more than just your savings—it's an investment toward your future. Being aware of the contribution deadlines will allow you to maximize your profit. You'll find that having a Roth IRA account does take a considerable amount of strategy. It is a little more thorough than having a standard liquid savings account that you can put money into whenever you feel like it. A Roth IRA account has rules in place that will help you become a more disciplined saver.

As mentioned earlier, the Roth IRA year is not a standard January through December. It operates on the same schedule as your typical tax year. This means that you have from January 1st until April 15th of the following year to make any contributions. Before your deadline on April 15th, you need to make sure that you have either contributed as much money as you can, maxed out your limit, or corrected any mistakes made by exceeding your limit. Just as April 15th has always been an important date because this is when your tax return is due, this will become important for another reason as soon as you have a Roth IRA account.

The deadline is April 15th, but you should always double-check to be sure you are on schedule. The money that you contribute up until this point is going to count for the present Roth IRA contribution year. This means that all of the limits and income information is going to apply from the rules set in the current year, even if you have already technically entered the next one. In some cases, you can extend this deadline if you extend your tax return deadline. Some people file for a six-month extension, which puts the new deadline on October 15th. If you choose to do this, it'll also apply to your Roth IRA contribution deadline.

If you're making your IRA contributions by check, you need to make sure that you place the appropriate year in the memo field. As mentioned, just because you might be in the next year does not mean that your contribution is already counted for that year. This is especially true if you file an extension, which allows you to make current contributions almost all the way through the following year. It sounds complicated at first, but if you remember how closely it follows the fiscal tax year, then you shouldn't have a problem remembering these important IRA deadlines.

To ensure that you are not missing out on any deadline, you should always double-check your eligibility requirements for the given year that applies. Remember that a change in income and age can impact the maximum amount that you are allowed to contribute. If you get a job that puts you in a higher income bracket, you will begin to phase out, and this can cause concerns about exceeding your contribution limit. You might also turn 60, which means that you will be able to contribute $7,000 instead of the standard $6,000 in the Roth IRA year. These guidelines are something that should be referenced often and regularly to make sure that you're within them.

It becomes disappointing when small mistakes are made that end up costing you money or preventing you from saving as much money as possible. You'll become an incredibly lucrative strategist once you get used to having a Roth IRA account. Everybody usually requires help in the beginning, but they tend to get the hang of it quickly. It all depends on how willing you are to do your research and to ask for help when necessary.

Withdrawal Rules and Penalties

You might need to withdraw from your Roth IRA account before you reach the age of retirement. There are several reasons why you might need to do this, but there is nothing to feel embarrassed or ashamed about. Because some people only keep a Roth IRA account as an emergency savings account, this is more common than you'd think. No matter what your personal situation is, you still need to learn about the rules and potential penalties involved if you do want to make a withdrawal.

The good news is that the rules surrounding withdrawals are pretty flexible! If you want to withdraw your contributions from your Roth IRA account, you can do so without any taxes or penalties. This can happen at any time, as well. Obviously, it makes more sense to keep the money in the account if you can because this is how you make it grow faster—through investments. There are some cases when you might need to take money out, though, and you should know that it's possible to do this fairly easily.

Your age impacts the rules surrounding withdrawals. If you are 59 ½, then you are able to withdraw both your contributions and earnings penalty-free and tax-free. This is under the assumption that the account is already five years old or older. If you are under this age, then you need to think smartly about the decision because there are a couple of exceptions to be aware of. While you can withdraw your contributions at any time, this is simply like taking back your original investment. If you are trying to buy a house for the first time or trying to pay for college expenses, the five-year rule does not apply. You should be able to have access to both your contributions and earnings in the account, however, you will still have to pay taxes on the earnings if you do this.

This is incredibly helpful because both of these major life events cost a lot of money. Keep in mind that you aren't going to have as much money in your Roth IRA account as someone who is 59 ½ because yours will be newer, but anything helps when you need the money to fund a large purchase. Not only are these very big purchases, but they are also investments that are being made toward your future. You can feel proud of yourself for being prepared for these moments!

If both you and your account are younger but you want to withdraw the earnings you have made with your Roth IRA, you can do this—just be prepared to face the penalties. These funds could be subject to a 10% penalty depending on how old you are and how long your account has been open. For some, this is worthwhile because an emergency might happen that leaves the individual with no choice. If you can help it, it's much better to keep the money in the account and allow it to grow for as long as you possibly can.

There are a couple of other exceptions that might help you avoid the 10% penalty. These include:

- Taking out a series of substantially equal distributions.
- You have unreimbursed medical expenses that total over 10% of your AGI.
- You're paying for medical insurance after losing your job.
- You're making a distribution due to an IRS levy.
- You need the money for disaster recovery.
- You're covering up to $5,000 of childbirth or adoption expenses.
- You're making a first-time home purchase.
- You're using the funds to pay for qualified higher education expenses.
- You become disabled or pass away.

If any of these situations apply to you, then you might not have to worry about your age or the five-year account age rules. It is always best to consult with your financial advisor before you do pull out any of the funds to make sure that you aren't going to be faced with hefty fees.

The main difference between withdrawing early and withdrawing after the five-year waiting period is that you will avoid only the 10% penalty upon an early withdrawal, but you will avoid both the 10% penalty and income tax on earnings if you wait until the account is past that five-year mark.

Why Maxing Out is Best

Maxing out means that you have made the maximum contribution allowed in the Roth IRA contribution year. Of course, this is a fantastic accomplishment because it not only means that you made enough money to make this contribution, but it also means that more money is going to be earning interest and being invested for future growth. Think about it this way—the more money you have to work with, the more potential you have to make it grow and the faster this can happen. Your goal should always be to max out, even if you do not think it is remotely possible.

Having big financial goals gives you something to work toward, and when you have them in mind, you will notice that you will start to make better financial decisions. Make it a goal of yours to max out your Roth IRA contribution amount, even if you have just opened the account this year. You might not get there on the first try, but you will get closer and closer with enough effort and persistence. If you want anything bad enough, you have to be willing to put in the hard work to get it.

The people who are able to max out their accounts are not only those in higher income brackets. They are people who make varying amounts of money or who might not even have a full-time job. The reason why they're able to do it is because of determination and discipline. If you are faced with a decision that provides instant gratification, you are likely to take it because everyone likes to see real-time results. This isn't how having a Roth IRA works, though.

You need to give it time before you can reap the rewards. If you think about the bigger picture, this isn't a negative thing.

You're probably familiar with the saying that the best things in life are worth waiting for, and this is something that definitely applies to a Roth IRA account. While you don't have to wait your entire lifetime to make a withdrawal, the longer you are able to wait and the more you are able to contribute, the better your results will be. Having an understanding that you plan on maxing out each year is going to motivate you to spend smarter and to think twice about those instant gratification expenses that you might not truly need.

Nobody wants to miss out on the fun or cool things in life, but you don't have to think about saving your money this way. Consider the future, not only this moment right now. Sure, you might buy a great new pair of expensive shoes that will be admired by your closest friends. What happens after they are worn-out and dingy? You'll have to get another pair, maybe something cheaper and sturdier because the other ones cost you a pretty penny. Thinking about this situation differently, what if you went with the functional shoes in the first place? You got what you needed, and you also put money away into your Roth IRA account for your future. This is a middle ground that you are able to meet with almost any tough purchasing decision. Sure, you might have to practice self-discipline, but maxing out your contribution is always going to be worth it!

Investing and Compounding

A Roth IRA account can be described as a part of your nest egg. This means that you're putting money aside to grow for you in case you need it. It's always recommended that everyone establish some type of nest egg if they can and to do so early in life. Because of the phenomenon of compounding, opening the account and beginning to invest as early as you are comfortable with will allow time to work in your favor. Even small investments that you make in the beginning can start to grow exponentially as time goes on. By the time you reach the age of retirement, you will have that peace of mind that you crave.

Terms like compounding can feel intimidating, but let's break it down with an example. Mary invests $100 in a selection of stocks and receives a 5% return. She reinvests the $5 she earned, meaning she now has $105 of stocks. The next time she receives her 5% return, it is calculated based on the $105 dollars she now has invested, meaning she earns $5.25. This might seem like a small change, but keep in mind that each time your investment compounds, you'll receive a greater return. This really builds up if you start investing early!

One additional aspect to keep in mind is that it's normal to see fluctuations in the value of your investments on a daily basis. It's important that you don't let this worry you, and you hold on to your investments and stick to your strategy. Over a period of years, you should see a positive return on your investment, especially if you started investing early and invested regularly throughout the years. We'll go more in-depth into exactly how you can invest using your Roth IRA account in the next chapter.

If you've been holding off on opening a Roth IRA account because you feel that you don't make enough money or you don't think investing is worthwhile, reconsidering this might change your perspective. Even a small sum of money, while invested properly, can grow to become a very healthy nest egg. It's also uplifting to know that you likely qualify for the account because of the broad income range requirements. When you start to apply these realities to your life, it should make you feel positive about your future. This is especially important in today's world where the status of the economy is not guaranteed to be healthy or predictable.

One feature of having a Roth IRA account that differs from having a standard liquid savings account is that you can select a beneficiary. This is a person who is entitled to the money if something were to ever happen to you. They will inherit the money after you die, and this can be helpful for so many reasons. Later in the book, the topic of how to select a beneficiary and why will be expanded on. It's not mandatory to select one, but it could make a lot of sense because your loved one will be able to accept the benefits of the nest egg that you worked hard to grow.

Some very important tax benefits might be lost if you do not select one, and it would be a shame to let this nest egg lose its positive, onward path toward growth. Be mindful that you can change your beneficiary. If you don't have children, you might decide to make your beneficiary your spouse or significant other. Life is unpredictable, so you might need to make changes in the future, and that is okay. Much like paying attention to your contribution limit, you should also be mindful of who your beneficiary is at all times.

4

START INVESTING IN YOUR ROTH IRA

The investment opportunities are a huge part of what makes a Roth IRA account so beneficial. When you contribute money, you have the potential to invest it in various ways, such as stocks and bonds. Even if you haven't invested money before, it is easy to do this through your Roth IRA account, and it is absolutely something that you should look into. This is how your money will grow exponentially because it all depends on how well your investments do. With any type of investing, there are naturally going to be risks involved, but this book will allow you to see that the process isn't complicated.

If you are interested in making investments with the money that you're contributing, you can open an investment account through establishments such as Vanguard or Fidelity, which you've probably heard of. These are not the only options, but they happen to be two of the most popular because of their ease of use. It only takes a minute to set up an investment account, and you can do this from the comfort of your own home online. If you already have an existing 401(k) plan through your employer, you probably have an investment account set up. For the sake of convenience, it's recommended that you open this new investment account for your Roth IRA with the same company to keep everything streamlined with your finances and investment opportunities.

In this chapter, we are going to take an in-depth look at why you should invest and how it's done. The thought of placing your money into stocks or bonds can sound very intimidating, but with guidance, you will gain the confidence necessary to make the best decisions with your contributions. As soon as you open your Roth IRA account and make a contribution, you can start investing—it's that easy!

Investment Flexibility

Having flexibility while making investments with your money is essential. With a Roth IRA account, you have this flexibility because you own the account. Through an employer-provided retirement account, there might be certain rules in place that limit you from investing in certain stocks or bonds. Having this type of financial freedom is refreshing. It shows you just how many options are available, and you have the time to think about what the smartest decision is for the hard-earned contributions that you're making.

When you start to enter the world of investments, mutual funds are something to become familiar with. They hold a lot of power and can help you grow your wealth in a very promising way. In the simplest terms, a mutual fund is an investment portfolio that is managed professionally. This means that you don't have to do the work of checking to see which options are most lucrative or how to reach a point where you feel that you're having success. What happens is that many investors pool money together within a mutual fund to invest in things that they deem worthy.

If you need a visualization—imagine that there are several people standing around a bowl that's empty. Each person takes $100 and places it into the bowl. Together, all of the people involved just mutually funded this pool of money that can now grow together. The term "mutual fund" can be taken quite literally, and you do not have to worry about not getting your fair share of the money. Because your money is managed professionally, it is the professional's job to keep track of how much you put into the bowl and how much you get out of the investment.

You might be curious about how many people invest this way, and the figures will tell you a lot—there are over 8,000 mutual funds in the United States (Hogan, 2020)! If you want to buy into a mutual fund, the process is simple. You can talk to your financial advisor about your desire to invest this way, and they'll let you know what your options are. This is yet another reason why having a professional on your side is going to help you stretch your dollar as much as possible. Most professionals advise that you should make it a goal to invest around 15% of your income for retirement, which can be quite a lot for some people (Hogan, 2020). Like maxing out your Roth IRA contribution, you don't have to hit this goal at the very beginning. Work your way up to it, and use it to give you the motivation and drive that you need.

Types of Investments

There are many types of mutual funds to look into when you are first starting out, but this is not the only way you can invest. As you know, there are also stocks and bonds that you can look into. These three are the most popular among investors who want to grow their finances, and they are the main ways that you can invest successfully through your Roth IRA account.

Target-Date Funds

A target-date fund is a mutual fund that is meant to grow your finances by a specific scheduled date. When you have a structured timeframe, you do not need to wait around wondering what is going on with your money and when you will reap the benefits. Most people will select their "target date" as their approximate age of retirement. Of course, this is a long-term option. If you wanted a shorter target date, you could also choose one. Some people use target-date funds to invest money for a child's future college expenses. It all depends on what is going on in your life and what you anticipate you will need this money for.

When you place your money into a target-date fund, it becomes more conservative over time. The reason this happens is that the growth of your investment is going to be gradual. This means that your professional advisor is going to take bigger risks by placing a larger portion of your investment in stocks at the beginning of your timeline. They know that you will need to have your money by the target date selected. Stocks offer a high potential for growth but no guarantees in the short-term due to the ever-changing market. This shift in target date funds is gradual, but they do tend to become more conservative than most investments by the time you're nearing the end of it. To put it simply, bonds offer security while stocks are risky.

As explained, investing in mutual funds is great because you do not have to put in any hard work after you make your initial investment. You will have someone to watch over your money and to make sure that it grows how you need it to grow. It's like you can enter auto-pilot as your money increases, which is a great feeling. Throughout the time that your money is in the target-date fund, it will periodically be reassessed to determine if it is still on the best path possible for you. Knowing that the smartest choices are being made for your given timeline will give you plenty of the peace of mind that you deserve.

Index Funds

An index fund is another type of mutual fund. This one differs from the target date fund because it is a mutual fund that is developed to track various components of a financial market index. An example is the Standard & Poor's 500 Index (S&P 500), which you may have heard of. An index fund is thought to give you a very broad market exposure with low operating expenses. The funds are meant to follow the benchmark of the index rather than the actual state of the market itself.

This means that even if a market is tanking, you do not have to worry too much about losing your entire investment. To most professionals, index funds are the ideal way to invest in mutual funds (Chen, 2020). They serve as a way for you to invest without having to hand-pick markets that you feel will give you the growth that you desire. It can become overwhelming to do things this way because it does require research.

When you invest in an index fund, this is known as taking a more passive investment strategy, which doesn't necessarily mean that it's a bad thing. If you don't have a set date that you need your money to grow by, then you can take your time with an index fund to see just how far your investment can take you. Since index funds essentially mimic the market, they are thought to outperform investing in a single company in the long run. This means that you are almost guaranteed to receive a return on your investment.

For nearly every market that exists, there is an index. When you invest in an index fund, your portfolio manager will build your portfolio so that its holding will mirror the securities of the particular index that matches. This is in their skill set and why it wouldn't be as easy for you to simply decide that you'd like to invest in an index fund on your own. You need this inside knowledge if you want to be successful.

Individual Stocks

There are pros and cons to all types of investments, and you have read a lot about the benefits of mutual funds so far. Another option that you do have with your Roth IRA account is the ability to invest in individual stocks. Even if you decide to do this, you aren't going to be on your own if you need help. A financial professional can still give you some guidance if you are unsure of which stocks are smart investments.

When you buy a stock, you will see a fee that you must pay. This is the only time any fees are involved. The longer that you keep the stock, the lower your cost of ownership is—ideally, you want to keep your shares for as long as you can, assuming the company is doing well. Buying stocks is one of the most straightforward ways you can invest with your Roth IRA account. You know exactly what you own and exactly which company you have invested in because you picked it out.

You are entirely in charge of the buying and selling process. If you notice that one company you've invested in is tanking, then you can make an immediate decision to either sell your shares or wait it out until it is on the up again and then sell your shares. Investing individually takes a lot of strategy, and this is something you'll learn once you begin buying stocks. Another great benefit of buying stocks is that it's easy to manage your taxes with them. As opposed to a mutual fund, individual stock investment puts you in full control of your gains and losses. When you have a mutual fund investment, the fund determines when to take your gains and losses, and they are also allowed to take a portion of your gains. Even if you just bought the fund at the end of the year, the mutual fund can still take their portion.

Investment Methods

To give you an even better idea of how you can personally invest the funds in your Roth IRA accounts, these methods will put everything into perspective for you. You'll be able to apply the strategies to your own life so you can truly visualize which option will work best. Of course, you can always run this information by your financial advisor, as well. Having as much knowledge as you can is going to give you the power to make the smartest investment decisions.

Method 1—Invest in a Target-Date Fund

If you are looking for the most convenient investment opportunity for your Roth IRA, this is the one you should select. It's also the best method for someone who doesn't want to constantly manage an investment portfolio on their own. In some ways, this method is like setting it and then forgetting about it because you have a manager on your side to keep an eye on things. It's also less costly than using a robo-advisor, which is a software meant to manage your portfolio with minimal human interaction. The robo-advisor will study algorithms and trends to make decisions for your investment. Again, this service can end up being pretty costly.

You should become familiar with the expression "funds of funds" because this is what a target date fund essentially is. In a target-date fund, your investment will typically be compared between three to five different indexes to determine the best output for your input. You'll see a wide variety of funds, including domestic stock, international stock, and international bonds. Given this broad variety, you are presented with what is known as an "asset allocation." This means that you will be able to see a percentage chart of where your funds are located and how they're doing.

A target-date fund is automatic, which means that it is not up to you to have to decide on the asset allocation portion of the investment. One factor that gets taken into consideration is your age. For example, the asset allocation for a 20-something college student who would like to buy a house one day is going to look different than a person who is in their 40s and nearing retirement age. To be even more specific, The Freedom Fidelity Index 2060 Fund is best for someone who is around 25-years-old. This fund gives you the amount of growth necessary if you are saving up this money for your future retirement in the year 2060 or a year that is close to it.

Again, you do not have to worry much about asset allocation because this is something that is automatically taken care of for you. The professional in charge of your portfolio can go over these decisions with you, but ultimately, they already have the knowledge necessary given your age, situation, and date that you set. This is why so many people opt for this type of investing—you truly just have to put the money into the investment and select a date! Getting to know more about target-date funds should put any past worries at ease. There is no complex stock market data that you are expected to learn and understand if you want to invest this way.

Of course, there are always downsides to any investment opportunity, and it's important that you consider them. One of the main downsides of a target date fund investment is that it is cookie-cutter, meaning that there is a standard template that is basically used for every investor. There's some degree of customization involved when it comes to your age and when you'd like to see your return, but the strategy is very simplified. Your age is a very big factor in this template because it tells your financial advisor what your risks are. This means they should be able to predict what your future expenses might be before retirement and which indexes will be a good fit based on these risks.

If you have any personal preferences in mind before you invest in a target-date fund, there isn't much you can do to apply this input. The system works automatically to prevent you from having to do this research. For some, this is a comforting thought. For others, they want more control. In an instance where you have a passion for only investing in companies that you deem ethically and personally fit to match your morals, you don't really have a choice. The portfolio manager is simply going to look at the figures, and then make the best decision based on the indexes they find.

This also poses a problem if you eventually decide you'd like to retire early. Since your target date is likely going to be set to an age closer to 60 than to 40, this is going to mean that you will not have your full return by that time if you do happen to get the opportunity to retire early. Overall, target-date funds are a good choice for most people, but of course, there are exceptions. Think about how much control you would personally like to have in the process, and also consider the possibility of you being able to retire early. If you trust in the direction of your portfolio manager and want something very convenient, this will still be a great option for you. Also, if you do not anticipate an early retirement, this can be great. There are some instances where things happen in your life that aren't predictable, but if you do not know about any of these right now, then investing in a target-date fund is a smart and fiscally responsible way to invest.

Method 2—Invest in Index Funds

An index fund differs from the "fund of funds" that the target date fund is made of. When you invest in an index fund, you actually get to have a say-so in which indexes you'd like to invest in. It is still less work than investing in individual stocks, but it gives you a little more control of where you want to put your money. An example of this is like going out to eat at a restaurant that allows you to customize your own pizza—they still cook it for you and provide the ingredients, but you get to tell them what to put on it. This seems a little less convenient than the previous method, but the benefit is that you have a little more control.

Some people do not care about having this control, and that is an entirely personal preference. For those who are just starting out in investing, taking the option that does everything for you automatically is probably going to seem a lot easier. Investing in an index fund seems to be a happy medium between investing in a target-date fund and purchasing individual stocks. It continues to showcase that you have a lot of options for your investments.

There are a lot of great benefits that you receive when you invest in an index mutual fund. For one, they are still managed by a professional that will guide your investment, even if you are the one who selects the specific index. You're never going to be on your own with that decision-making process. Also, they can be very diverse. Once you do a little research, you will see just how many indexes there are and why they could be a great fit for you and your investment. Lastly, they are cost-efficient. The entire point of making an investment is to grow your finances, not to deplete them. Nobody wants to end up losing money because of a bad investment choice.

The first step to buying index funds is to decide on your asset allocation. Where do you actually want your money to go? Take the time to really research all of the possibilities that you have before you make this decision because it's an important one. Stocks always encourage growth—you've probably heard plenty about the stock market being "on the rise," whereas bonds are more stable because they don't fluctuate like stocks. If you are seeking fast growth, choosing stocks would make sense. With the main goal of stability, investing in bonds is probably smarter. This all comes down to risk versus reward! You need to determine what your priorities are with your investment. When you are younger, you probably want to invest in stocks because you have more time to save up for retirement. This can also be an exciting process to delve into.

Jack Bogle's Recommended Portfolio Allocation

Jack Bogle, the founder of Vanguard, has a method for asset allocation that is easy to understand and to manage. He suggests minimal rebalancing of your portfolio, once annually being enough. It can be tempting to want to rebalance every other month, especially if you aren't seeing the growth you desire, but patience is key. He also states that you probably shouldn't invest directly overseas. Bogle does this simply because he likes to invest in what he knows best. This is already a learning experience, so investing directly overseas can complicate things for you. There are different rules and trends to learn. Diversification is also mentioned in Bogle's strategy.

This is similar to diversifying your credit portfolio—if you have credit cards, a mortgage, and a car loan, this is going to actually boost your score rather than only having one type of financial debt. Bogle says that an easy way to diversify your portfolio is to invest in some bonds. As mentioned, these are stable, and they should not hinder you. He also mentions that making things as simple as possible will lessen your worry. If you make a lot of complex and uneducated decisions about your investments, you will end up being concerned about it—this is natural. Take away the stress by keeping it as simple as you can.

His method can also be calculated with a formula that he came up with:

100 minus your age = stock allocation

Once you put that amount into stocks, you can put the remaining percentage toward bonds. This makes it simple, as he advises. For example, if you are 25 right now, you would invest 75% into stocks and 25% into bonds.

David Swenson's Recommended Portfolio Allocation

If you are the type of person who doesn't care to place all of your eggs in one basket, take David Swensen's strategy into consideration. Swensen is infamously known as the manager of Yale's $30B endowment fund. He carefully allocates his funds into several different investments, providing him many opportunities for growth. This is his formula:

Domestic Stocks - 30%

Foreign Stocks - 15%

Emerging Market Stocks - 5%

REITs (Real Estate Investment Trusts) - 20%

US Treasury Bonds - 15%

US Treasury Inflation Protection Securities - 15%

What Swenson has done here with his funds is spread them out in a way that is meant to withstand any economic status. He is protecting himself, his assets, and his future by spreading his money out. Of course, this is a more complex method of asset allocation, but if you like the look of this method, you can always bring this up with your financial advisor to see what can be done with the funds you're working with.

To further break down why Mr. Swenson allocates his funds this way, it is important to understand the benefits of these investments. Typically, stocks and real estate always do well in any given market. Treasury inflation protection is something that will also be a great performer. If the economy experiences a recession, this is when bonds shine.

Beginner Advice

There is a lot to learn about index funds, and this is because you can benefit greatly if you work smartly. As a beginner, it is suggested that you find low-cost index funds. You can do this by looking at the expense ratio. This expense ratio is basically an annual fee that will get taken out of your investment as a percentage. If you find a low-cost index with a high expense ratio, you might end up losing out on your investment because of this annual fee. Aim to find an expense ratio that is under 0.20%. This will put you on the safe side.

Once you find some funds that are suitable, you can begin to build your asset allocation. If you are still relatively young, it is a good idea to have a 70:30 ratio of stocks to bonds. This means, if you have $100 to put into your Roth IRA, you should put $70 into stocks and $30 into bonds. The reason being is because stocks can grow a lot faster, as bonds tend to be more stagnant. If your main goal is to see a lot of growth, you can consider doing a 100% stock allocation in the beginning.

Method 3—Invest in Individual Stocks

If you're seeking the most DIY way to invest, go for individual stocks. However, remember that investing in individual stocks means that you'll have to do a lot of research on each one. Not only do you have to track its performance, but you also need to make sure that each company aligns with your morals, beliefs, and goals. This is also a method that requires maintenance, as stocks can change daily. While you might be having a great run with some of your stocks, this could change in an instant. This doesn't necessarily mean that you need to reinvest these funds, though. The point is that you need to look at the trends and see what is most likely to happen next. Investing in stocks is kind of like playing chess; you always need to be thinking one step ahead in your strategy.

It is possible to do this in the beginning, but it is a rare approach unless you have some prior investment knowledge. Plus, you need to consider diversification, which is the allocation of your money into different types of investments. If you are only investing in stocks, then when the stocks crash, your money will stop growing. These are just some factors to keep in mind, as the decision is still entirely up to you. Once you find a company that you think you'd like to invest in, perform a financial check-up on them. You can do this by using a tool like Morningstar to track how much debt the company is in and what their current financial standing is. There are a few other key points to look at:

Interest Coverage Ratio =

Earnings Before Interest (EBIT) / Interest Expense

An interest coverage ratio above two is considered acceptable. You want this number to be higher because this means that the company is less burdened with interest.

Debt-to-assets Ratio = Total Debt / Total Assets

Most agree that the ratio should not rise above 2.0. When you are looking at larger companies, such as manufacturers, you'll notice that their ratio will probably be higher than 2.0 because of the equipment and supplies used to make their business run.

Payback Period = Initial Investment / Yearly Cash Flow

When you invest in stocks, you shouldn't expect a fast return. You need to let your money stay in the market long enough to grow. As you look at the payback periods of various companies, try to aim for the ones that are three years or less. If you wait any longer, you might be investing in a company with debt, which you don't want.

The next step is to take a look at the company's profitability. Of course, you want a company that you can see is on the rise. If you notice a downward spiral trending, this is not a company likely to provide you with a positive end result. Take a look at their EPS (earnings per share); you want this to showcase a strong upward trend. Also, look at the ROIC (return on invested capital). You should aim for 10% or higher on this.

Finally, see if the stock is being traded at a reasonable rate. To do this, follow this formula:

$$\textit{Price-to-Earnings Ratio} =$$
$$\textit{Stock Price/EPS (earnings per share)}$$

You can see all of this information from your investment account, and with some calculations, you'll be able to determine if it's being traded reasonably. If you can see that the price of the stock costs way more than the earnings that shareholders are getting, it's safe to say that you should steer clear of investing your money with them. Generally, a good way to determine if the price-to-earnings ratio is good is if it is 15 or less.

5

MANAGING YOUR PORTFOLIO

Once you have a Roth IRA account in place, you do need to think about portfolio management strategies. Many people opt to have a professional assist them with this part, but it's definitely not mandatory. If you feel more comfortable self-managing, you can go with this option.

This chapter will cover the pros and cons of both and the important factors that must be observed. Because investing requires attention to detail, it does help to have another set of eyes present to spot any opportunities or potential losses. This is your money, so you must be very careful with it if you want to see it grow at its maximum potential.

Rebalancing

The term "rebalancing" is the process of reviewing your investments' performance and redistributing the money in your portfolio to make sure you're on track toward your financial goals. In some cases, rebalancing can mean buying or selling stocks because you can see that the trends have changed. Maybe you or your advisor will find something that looks like it'll create a better turnout. Using this as an example—imagine that Jane originally set up an asset allocation that consists of 50% stocks and 50% bonds. After a few months, she takes a look at her portfolio to see how her money is doing and if it is growing at the rate expected. During this time, her stocks performed very well, making her portfolio reflect a 70% success rate with the stocks. She then decided that she wanted to change her asset allocation, and she changed her portfolio to reflect a 70/30 ratio that favors stocks. Given time, certain markets began to crash, and she could see that she was losing money. After Jane noticed, she decided that she wanted to make her portfolio reflect her original 50/50 goal.

To do this, Jane would sell some of her stocks and buy more bonds, getting her back on track with the original plan that she laid out. It might seem counterproductive to do this if the stocks are doing so well, but this is an optimal time to sell stocks because this means she will definitely be getting a return on the investment. That is new money earned and new money that can be used for Jane's future. Remember, stocks are more unpredictable; they can change daily. Bonds are more conservative. After rebalancing her portfolio, the same thing might happen again in a few months, and she will have another win when it comes to receiving a return on her investments.

Essentially, rebalancing your portfolio serves as a safeguard for your investments. If you put a pie in the oven for the amount of time recommended but never come back to check on it, there's still a chance it will burn. You can think of your investment portfolio in the same way—just because you have a goal in mind and go through all of the right steps does not 100% guarantee you'll receive the desired outcome. Another benefit of rebalancing your portfolio, assuming you have an advisor helping you, is that the advisor can stay on a path that they know best. They'll be able to determine which moves are risky and which moves are going to benefit you. Any time someone is knowledgeable about a topic, it makes sense that they'd stay within their area of expertise.

If you are investing in even just one single stock, this is going to change the way that your portfolio is balanced because the stock market is guaranteed to change. Even if you do not fully understand Wall Street and its workings, you probably know that reports are given on a daily basis to inform investors of how every stock is performing. There are many things that can impact stock exchange rates, such as the financial status of the company or consumer needs. For example, many more people have been signing up for digital media subscriptions in the last decade as compared to the decades before when cable companies ruled television. Almost everyone you know probably has a Netflix, Hulu, Prime, or other subscription.

If you were invested in a cable company, you might rebalance your portfolio to discover that there are other companies that are in much higher demand, such as the digital providers mentioned above. It'd probably be a smarter investment move to pay attention to this trend and to get some of your money into that stock since it has more potential to grow. Then, check on it again in the next few months. See how well it is performing and see how much it changed the balance of your portfolio. The stock market revolves around a constant process of buying and selling, even when your stocks are at their best. This is how you make money.

In the earlier example, Jane had a 50/50 balance with her portfolio, but this isn't mandatory. Your balance can be anything you'd like it to be, from 70/30 to 40/60. What matters most is that you are paying attention to your portfolio to ensure that it's staying within this balance. If you discover that it isn't, then it's time for a rebalance. You can either choose to do this yourself or have an advisor help you make these decisions. Even if someone else is managing your portfolio, you still get a say in where your money goes, and you can still do your own research if you choose. A financial advisor is there to help answer your questions about good investments and bad investments.

There isn't a particular schedule you have to stick to when it comes to rebalancing your portfolio, but you should at least aim to rebalance once annually. This will give you a good idea of what is going on, though some choose to rebalance more frequently. Nothing extremely negative would happen if you don't rebalance your portfolio, but you might be missing out on investment opportunities simply because of the fact that you or an advisor is not looking into them. It is not recommended to never rebalance your portfolio. Many people like to start out with a financial advisor, especially in the beginning. They'll be able to guide you through the process, and they'll let you know when they think is the best time for you to personally rebalance your portfolio since they'll be keeping an eye on it.

With rebalancing, you need to find what is most comfortable for you. Once annually is good, but checking every few months is also great. Weekly would probably be excessive. Depending on what you decide to do, even if your portfolio is managed by someone else, you can give them your preference on this. Don't be afraid to be vocal about your portfolio and to ask any questions that arise. Remember, this is your money and the risks involved directly impact you! It is not overbearing to ask plenty of questions or to want to stay in the loop. That is what a financial advisor is there to help you do.

Financial Advisors

A financial advisor is there to help give you advice on what to do with your finances—a crucial part of the investment process when you have a Roth IRA account. You may have some ideas of how you'd like to invest your money, but an advisor can help you make a plan that will actually get you the results you are striving for. It will give you peace of mind knowing that you are not alone during this process because it might be new to you. Understand that your advisor is there to answer any of your questions, no matter how obvious they may seem to you—nothing is too insignificant when it comes to the safety and security of your money.

A financial advisor is someone who is licensed to give you this advice and must carry a license known as the Series 65 if they are conducting business with the public. You can always do your research on your advisor to ensure they're properly licensed. There are also many other licenses a financial advisor can hold if they specialize in certain areas of expertise. Financial advisors do not only help to manage investments. They can help you with tax planning, estate planning, and insurance shopping. When you hire one, you are actually getting a plethora of services.

When you hire a financial advisor, it makes sense to hire one that works for the establishment that you hold your investment account with. This person is already going to know the way that your account and portfolio works, so you won't have to question their knowledge. It is also a lot more convenient to be able to go to one single place to take care of all your financial investment needs. Hiring one is simple, and you will probably be offered the option once you open your investment account. If not, you can always ask somebody who works there what your options are.

If you are wary about financial advisors taking advantage of your lack of financial knowledge, consider hiring a fee-only fiduciary advisor. Fiduciary advisors are obligated to give financial advice in your best interest. This is because they are not motivated by commissions for selling insurance or investment products. Instead, they are considered "fee-only" because they are funded solely by you—the client they need to satisfy in order to keep you on board. It's helpful to directly ask a fiduciary advisor to provide curated financial advice specific to your needs.

Some places where you can hire a fiduciary advisor include Vanguard, SmartAsset, and E*Trade. This is helpful to know if you do not yet have an investment account set up and if you do not want to go through your standard bank. These are among the top three places where individuals usually manage their investments because the companies are reputable and experienced. They handle portfolios of all sizes for people in all walks of life. You don't need to assume that you do not qualify for a fiduciary advisor just because you are just starting out with your Roth IRA account or because you're already pretty close to the retirement age.

Much like opening your Roth IRA account in the first place, you don't need to assume that you're ineligible for fiduciary services. Anyone can use them, even those who do not have their IRA account set up yet. Some opt to hire one beforehand so they can get a better idea of what investment options they have—it all depends on what you feel most comfortable with. Throughout this entire process, listen to your instincts. This is your money that you are dealing with, so you should feel confident with every move you make regarding your asset allocation choices.

Another option to be aware of is a financial broker. This is basically a person who acts as your middleman if you are planning on buying and selling a lot of stocks. They will do all of the work and research for you based on your requests, but they get a commission on your returns. This means that you do not get to keep your full investment return, but it might be a worthy option given how much research and time it takes to fully understand the stock market. Most people don't have the time to sit down and watch it daily, let alone learn all of the calculations and percentages necessary to make smart investment decisions.

A stockbroker is a title you've probably heard many times. You might be most familiar with the term when talking about Wall

Street and the stock exchange, but they provide services for individuals, as well. There are brokers who work for big companies like the ones mentioned above, but there are also independent brokers who work for smaller firms if you feel too intimidated to place your trust in someone who works for a multi-million-dollar establishment. While there's absolutely nothing wrong or bad about either decision, it all comes down to your personal preference.

Something else that you can look into is hiring an investment advisor. This individual, or group, is mainly there to give you advice. They will make an analysis of your portfolio, and then they will let you know what your best options are. Typically, you'll still do the work from investing in the stock market to buying the mutual funds. This is sort of a middle ground that you can choose if you'd like to have someone to give you advice yet still want most of the control over your finances.

Knowing who to trust with your money is a big decision, and it's also personal. Whether you decide to take a more independent route or hire someone to manage your finances in the background, do what you think is best for you. However, if you don't know where to start, it's best to start with a fiduciary advisor because they will guide you from point A to point B without a lot of work on your end. They also might end up teaching you a lot about the various investment markets, and this knowledge will come in handy later on if you do decide to invest more independently.

Self-management

If you're thinking of managing your investment portfolio on your own—you're not alone! Many people do take this route just because of the personal nature of the entire process. It isn't impossible, but it does take some relatively careful planning and a lot of research if you'd like to make the best decisions for your money. All of the same data and news about the stock market and various funds/indexes are available at your fingertips. You can read about all of this information online, and there is no secret guidebook that a fiduciary investor has that you won't. The only thing that they will have is a license and more immediate knowledge about the topic, but that isn't to say that you can't get to a point where you have plenty of knowledge about it yourself.

There have been many studies done on self-management versus having your portfolio managed by a professional, and the results are naturally quite different. It has been shown that individual investors still do not perform as well simply because they don't know the markets as well as the professionals do (Smith, 2019). Remember, financial advisors do this for a living. They are trained to work with the markets, and they do this on a daily basis. When you take on the task, you are essentially taking on a very time-consuming hobby. Again, that's not to say it's impossible.

A particular study run by DALBAR from 1990 to 2010 showed that the S&P 500 index earned 7.81% annually. For those who decided to go in as individual investors, they were only earning around 3.49% annually (Smith, 2019). This is a huge difference, and it shows just how much of a return they could have made if they had used a different strategy or sought help from a professional. Overall, it depends on what your priorities are. Do you want your money to grow as much as possible as quickly as possible? Most would answer yes to this question, so the answer seems pretty clear as to the results you'll find if you decide to self-manage your portfolio.

To give you an example based on the study, over the course of 20 years, a $100,000 investment would grow to almost $450,000 if taken to its full potential with the help of an advisor or other strategy. That same $100,000 investment would only grow to $198,000 over 20 years while taking the self-management approach. You can see that this is a staggering difference, and while you wouldn't have lost out on your investment, this still isn't great for a 20-year timeframe. The study suggests that the problem with self-management is that you get your emotions involved, which is natural because you are seeing your money either grow or decline.

When an individual investor saw that a market was going down, they'd immediately move their funds out of instinct into a market that was doing well. This seems like a natural decision to make, but is it the smartest one? When you sell your stock to get out of a market while it's at its lowest, you are getting the lowest return. You may even end up losing money on your original investment. A big strategy involves waiting out these market lows and only selling when the market is more lucrative. Even if you can see in the trends that the market isn't doing well, it can still fluctuate. You'll want to move your money then rather than when it is at its very lowest potential for growth.

You can probably see that one of the common problems made through self-management are rookie mistakes. This is something that anyone could have done out of instinct, but it isn't necessarily the right strategy to use while investing money. You always want to come out on top, even if this means waiting. Another thing is that it can be very hard to remain patient as you see your stocks crashing. Your instincts might be screaming at you to move your money, but when it comes to the stock market, you have to wait it out and see what happens next. Also, being one step ahead of the trends through a lot of studying is going to be very beneficial to you.

This book is meant to give you all of the options available to you, so this is still one to think about, even after hearing about the studies and the warnings. Some people are just naturally more independent and emotionally-driven, and that's okay. If you'd like to try it, you can remember that it isn't a permanent decision that you have to stick with. If it ever becomes too hard or time-consuming, you can still hire a fiduciary advisor to get you back on track and to help you reach your goals.

Investment Methods

You've learned a lot about portfolio management in this chapter, and it's understandable if it's a lot to digest. Because you have so much freedom with your Roth IRA, you'll often be faced with these decisions that you must make, even if you do end up hiring someone to help you with your investments. Now, we are going to compare the pros and cons of each so you can have a side-by-side analysis of what option looks best for you right now. Remember, the option that you think is best right now can change. Whether it changes in a year from now or a month from now, you'll always have the ability to take a new approach if you think it'd be better. Reassure yourself that you are never going to be boxed into a corner with financial investments because many people see it as an all-or-nothing process. In reality, your Roth IRA investments can be quite flexible.

Financial Advisor Pros and Cons

Pros:

• You will always have someone to contact if you have any questions or concerns about your monetary investments. Even if you feel the question is irrelevant, it's not going to be a problem for your advisor to sit down with you and ensure that you are feeling confident in your decisions.

• You have someone you can bounce ideas off of, even if they are the ones managing your portfolio. Maybe you have noticed some trends that you find promising—this would be a great opportunity to let your advisor know to see what they think about it.

• If you don't want to have to think about your investments, you have the ability to place your money into the various funds, indexes, and stocks, and then forget about it. Your advisor is going to be keeping a close watch on everything for you so that you can resume your already busy life.

Cons:

• You have less control over what is going on with your money. At any given time, your advisor might be making changes that you do not necessarily know about or agree with.

• It usually costs some sort of fee to have an advisor on your side, and this is especially true with someone like a stockbroker who receives a cut of your earnings.

• You might feel overwhelmed with all of the options that you have on who to hire and which establishment to use. Just because you bank at one location does not mean you must hire your advisor from the same one. It becomes difficult to know who's going to be the best fit for your financial goals.

Self-management Pros and Cons

Pros:

• You have complete control and freedom over everything that goes on with your asset allocation. It can feel exhilarating to know that you have this much financial freedom when it is usually the opposite feeling in any other situation that involves your money.

• When you do enough research, you might end up realizing that you have a true passion for keeping up with the markets and trends. You can catch on very quickly, and all of the information you'll need is easily accessible online.

• You will not have to share your earnings with anyone once you receive them. Because there is no middleman or advice-giver, you don't have to worry about cutting them a portion of what you have worked so hard to get back in return.

Cons:

• Doing adequate research to make smart investment decisions is time-consuming. It can also be very confusing. You'll need to make this a part of your regular routine if you truly want to master the stock market and all of its trends.

• You are more likely to make rookie mistakes simply because it isn't your job to invest money. These small mistakes can end up being very costly in the long run, and you might be missing out on big return opportunities.

• When you self-manage, you have to look at your investment portfolio a lot. It isn't something that you can just let sit there and grow on its own. You'll have to make proactive decisions when you see that the markets are changing.

No matter which option you choose, you now have a great comparison of both that includes all of the pros and cons. Study this list widely, and see which option feels best for you at the moment. You can always refer back to this list if you are unsure or if you end up changing your mind.

6

MAX OUT YOUR RETIREMENT ACCOUNTS

It has been mentioned earlier in the book but maxing out your retirement accounts is ultimately the most beneficial action you can take. This chapter will break down how and why, answering all of your questions on how to make this goal a reality. When you max out your Roth IRA account, this means you have made the maximum contribution for the year. More money in the account means more chances for it to grow into larger wealth. Saving money can be difficult, especially when special occasions like the holidays come around. You may be tempted to withdraw your contributions from your Roth IRA to fund certain purchases. Even though you can withdraw your contributions at any time without penalty, you should think of the account as an emergency-only fund.

Ask yourself if this purchase is going to serve a temporary, recreational purpose or if it's necessary because of a serious situation. Getting into the mindset of saving money is difficult, even for those who are generally good at it. Saving money takes a lot of self-discipline, and having a Roth IRA can encourage you to grow these traits in yourself. Try your best to remember that your ultimate goal is to max out by the end of the year. As you see yourself getting closer, you will feel a sense of pride that's irreplaceable. Not to mention, you'll also receive monetary gain!

Which Takes Priority? 401(k) or Roth IRA?

This might be your first experience with having a Roth IRA account, but it is great to consider any other retirement accounts you have in place at the moment. If you work full-time and have an employer-provided retirement plan, this is something else that you can benefit from. Find out if your 401(k) plan has the employer match feature. This means that any contributions you make will be matched by your employer, quickly growing your funds. It's a great benefit of having this type of 401(k) plan, and some people aren't even aware of it because they don't look into it.

Making sure that you're doing your due diligence when you have any type of retirement account is important. Ask to see the initial paperwork that you signed if you can't remember the terms of your 401(k). Alternatively, you can also ask a boss or a supervisor to sit down with you and go over these terms. You can find out how much money it takes to max out your 401(k) account within the year because this is also possible, just like having a Roth IRA account.

Something else to consider is that you should try to max out your 401(k) plan first. One reason is because of the employer-matched contributions. If you have these, this money is going to grow quickly, and you will be able to max out a lot faster than if you were only focusing on your Roth IRA, which is not going to be matched. Once you max out your 401(k) plan, you will have that extra money to contribute to your Roth IRA account. This is a recommended strategy if you have multiple accounts that you are trying to max out by the end of the year. Always go for the one that has the quickest growth first because this will allow you to get closest to that maximum contribution.

Depending on the salary that you make, your 401(k) maximum contribution limit should be pretty similar to your Roth IRA maximum limit. In some cases, the limit can be slightly higher than that of a Roth IRA account. This information combined with employer-match allows you to quickly contribute a lot of money to the account while efficiently maxing out. You end up being able to put away more for your nest egg if you make your 401(k) your primary focus. Once you are able to do this, you can then shift your priority to any other secondary accounts that you have.

Take Advantage of Compounding Interest

You already know about the Roth IRA's interest-earning feature, but did you also know that there is another feature that makes your money grow even faster? The phenomenon of compound interest. When you max out your contribution and invest it, you are allowing yourself to take advantage of as much compound interest as you can. Each time that your investment works in your favor, meaning the investment earns you interest, that money gets added into your account and now can earn even more interest. With all of the right investment moves, you could be making millions! By the end of each year, maxing out is super important because this gives you the chance to truly grow your money at an impressive rate.

There are many factors to consider how much your money will grow numerically, and one of these factors is the diversity of your portfolio. Since you can invest in stocks, bonds, funds, and more, this provides you with several different ways to ensure that your money is working its hardest for you while it's in your Roth IRA account. While you still may be a little unsure of how you plan on investing, making this plan early on to diversify your account is going to work well in your favor.

Taking a real-life example, if you were to contribute the full $6,000 contribution limit and then invest it in a variety of different markets, this gives you the potential for your money to experience several different kinds of growth. Maybe one of the stocks you selected is having a great year and is on the uprise—this can lead to double the original investment that you put in! This means that your $6,000 can realistically turn into $12,000. Imagine if you spread your investments into several different markets that all turned out to be very successful this year. What this means for you is a very healthy savings account that can double, triple, or even quadruple.

Another factor to consider on the topic of compounding is how soon you plan on retiring. If you are young, then this means you have a lot of time for your money to sit in the account and grow. While keeping a diverse portfolio the entire time and experiencing great success with your returns, this growth will continue to happen for you year after year. If you calculate the numbers, you'll easily recognize that your money has a lot of potential. This is why Roth IRA accounts have a lot more advantages than traditional liquid savings accounts, where you only rely on a small amount of growth due to an interest rate.

For an average person with a regular savings account, this interest rate probably isn't going to be very much. You might earn anywhere from a few cents to a few dollars by the end of each year, depending on how much is in the account and how high your interest rate is. While this is still growth, it isn't the kind of growth you need if this is your nest egg for retirement. A Roth IRA account with investments truly sets the bar a lot higher if you think about it.

One term you must familiarize yourself with is "risk tolerance." This basically translates to how many risks you are willing to take to receive big rewards. If you are about to max out your Roth IRA with a $6,000 contribution yet you only invest in bonds, you know that this will result in conservative growth. It's still going to be more than the average liquid savings account provides, but it won't have quite the same impact as if you were to invest in stocks and mutual funds simultaneously. Honestly, a lot of this has to do with experimentation and practice. You need to feel out the markets and determine what your risk tolerance is, what you are most comfortable investing in, and how much you'd like to invest.

Your risk tolerance is sort of like your intuition, but you combine it with your knowledge of the markets. If you have an advisor to help you, they'll be able to assist you in determining what your risk tolerance is. They might even encourage you to make moves that are riskier than you thought possible, yet the payout will prove that they're worthwhile. Feel out each situation, and make sure that you fact-check as much as possible. Even when you have an advisor to help you, remember that you can also check on the stats of any market at any time online. Do your research if you feel it's necessary.

Another real-life example of a Roth IRA return while maxing out is that, statistically, you are supposed to get around 7-10% back on your investments each year (Chorpenning, 2019). Doing the math, this means that you can make around $83,000 in 10 years alone! It's a wonderful possibility to consider, and it's a reality that can really happen with your investments. If you max out your account and think about the next 30 years, this can mean you might accumulate around $500,000. That's half a million dollars! These possibilities are exciting, and they should make you feel motivated to invest.

Comparing and contrasting this information is important. If you were to keep that $6,000 in a liquid savings account, assuming you are only relying on your interest rate and contributing $6,000 a year, you'd end up with the sum total of your contributions ($60,000) and a few hundred dollars earned in interest. While this is still an impressive sum, it doesn't compare to the possibility of earning $83,000 with a Roth IRA account. You always have to think about the bigger picture, that one day you'll be using these funds during your retirement. It makes sense to have a desire to save up as much as you can, so you'll be set for your future. Not to mention, you also give your family a greater degree of security, as well.

If you'd like to calculate the growth of your personal contributions, there are websites online that can help you by taking the numbers that you input and the investments that you've made. They'll multiply the money for you so you can get an idea of what to expect in 10, 20, and even 30 years' time. Roth IRAs help you think about these factors, and it's important to start thinking about them as early as you can. Being realistic and smart with your money is something that can change your entire lifestyle. The sooner you are willing to invest and make maxing out your Roth IRA account a priority in life, the sooner you'll see the exponential growth that you crave.

Market Highs and Lows

When you invest in any market, no matter how large or reputable it is, there isn't a guarantee that you will see growth throughout the entire year. Consider how much can change in a single month, let alone a whole year. Consumer needs change, the economy changes, and several other factors all fall into place that determine how the market you've invested in will pay out. There are a couple of strategies you can use to reduce the impact of market fluctuations on your investments.

One option you can try is called dollar-cost averaging. This strategy involves investing a moderate amount on a regular basis, such as every month or even every week if you'd like. Using this method, even if you are sometimes making investments when the market is high and your investments are "expensive", you'll be equally likely to make your investments when the market is low and your investments are "cheap". Thus, as you keep investing throughout the year, you are able to average out fluctuations in the market and let your investments grow.

However, dollar-cost averaging isn't the right strategy for everyone. If you have a large amount of money available to invest at once, you might miss out on returns and growth in the market if you invest it over a long time period instead of all at once. In this case, you may decide to do some market research and make your investments once you feel the prices are at a low point early on in the year. This way you can take advantage of the growth that happens in the market throughout the rest of the year. Also, if you aren't able to invest regularly or on a schedule, don't fret! Do some research each time you have money to invest so that you can choose investments you expect will perform well.

If you see that your investment isn't doing very well for a period of time, this is not an automatic sign that you've made a bad choice and need to sell your investments. As previously mentioned, selling your shares when a market is at a low point means that you aren't going to get very much back for them. It might even result in you losing money because the payout is so low. Instead, look at past fluctuations in the market or industry you've invested in and try to predict whether your investments will recover. Most likely, you're just observing a cyclical trend. For example, activewear brands tend to increase in value during warmer months and decrease during cold weather when less people are active.

This is part of the risk tolerance aspect that was mentioned earlier; you need to figure out how much risk you are comfortable with and willing to take on. Even though investing in stocks is considered a riskier approach than investing in bonds, you can still be conservative with your strategy. If you want to go for markets that you know will likely see year-round growth, think about the products or services that people cannot live without. Markets that revolve around resources can usually provide you with some security because they aren't as seasonal as others. This is another reason you should try to invest closer to the beginning of the year—you can capitalize on this growth.

Feeling unsure about this decision is normal and natural. Most people dislike taking risks with money, especially money that has the potential to grow. You can combat this fear by using the strategies we discussed above and minimizing the impact of market fluctuations on your investments. By doing so, you'll be able to make the smartest decisions for your investments, and you'll feel proud of your achievements. It also goes to say that you should not automatically celebrate when you invest in a market that is continually on the rise.

A market that is performing well won't necessarily have a crash the very next day, but it is possible for it to experience a downward trend. The most important takeaway while researching markets is that you cannot guarantee anything about them—it's almost like a gamble, but it's more secure because of the research that you put into it or because of the knowledge that your advisor already has. This allows you to make predictions and invest strategically, which can give you some peace of mind as you figure out what to do with your contributions.

Why You Shouldn't Wait Till Tax Day

When you have a lot of time to complete a task, you are more likely to forget about it. Since the Roth IRA contribution year follows the same schedule as the tax year, you might forget about it in the beginning only to wait until the last minute to make your maximum contribution. These mistakes can happen, but there are many reasons why you should not wait. For one, it's a great idea to get into the habit of saving money on a weekly basis. When you build up these good habits, they are more likely to stick with you in the future. Before making any purchases or spending any extra money you have, think about what else you might be able to do with these funds.

If you want to create a good habit in your life, you need to commit to it. Put money aside daily! This sounds impossible to some, but you can likely put away one dollar every single day that can go into your savings account. When you think about things from this perspective, you'll see how quickly one dollar can turn to seven within a week. Within a month, that's 30 dollars that you didn't have saved up before. Of course, this is a very modest goal. You need to create goals that challenge you. The ones that seem impossible are the ones that you'll feel more motivated to pursue.

Don't forget the difference between your liquid savings account and your Roth IRA account. If you put your money into your regular account, you may forget about it and end up losing out on the potential to invest this money. While keeping a close eye on your contribution limit and what you have already put in, it's a better idea to put your savings into your Roth IRA first. There are no additional risks involved because you can still withdraw the contribution in case of an emergency just as you can with a regular savings account. The difference is the possibility of exponential growth while in the Roth IRA.

For the sake of remembering that you do have this wonderful opportunity in front of you, get into the habit of checking your bank balances every few days or at the end of each week. This is something you might already do, and if so, continue! This is a great habit because it makes you aware of how much money you actually have, how much your money is growing, and how well you are doing on your savings plan. Some banks even allow you to put in figures that represent your goals. They'll make charts and graphs for you that show you how close you are. For those who enjoy visual representation, this can come across as very motivating.

Missing Out on Growth

If you don't have money in your Roth IRA account at the beginning of the year, you are missing out on one of the biggest features of the account—its compounding growth. Without money to invest, there is no possibility of growth. Imagine that you wait until the month of April to place your contribution into your account. While it might be the maximum contribution, which is great, this only gives you a few weeks of time to invest it. Given the example, the money will probably not grow very much. In a sense, it's like you simply put it into a regular savings account.

Just as you plan on filing your taxes every year, you know that you shouldn't wait until April 14th to start working on them. Most people begin early on in January, February, or March—the sooner the better. You can think of your Roth IRA contribution in the same way. You need to start contributing early on so you have time to invest, otherwise, you are just selling yourself short. Your money will be in the account, but it won't be working hard for you like you know it can. To master this, all it takes is some self-discipline and motivation. Keep your goals in mind at all times.

Being able to see a list of all that you want to do in life can help remind you to set money aside. Envision what you are going to do after you retire. With all of your spare time, you will probably want to travel and explore places you've never been to before. To do this, you need money. Think about all there is for you to see and discover, possibly even print out photos of these places to put on a vision board so you will always be reminded of your future goals. Maybe you don't wish to travel, but you do wish to renovate your home into your dream home. You can make a vision board of the ideal house of your dreams.

Missing the Market Highs

Another reason why you shouldn't wait until the last minute to invest your money is that you are missing out on the majority of market growth that will occur. You know that the market is unpredictable—it experiences highs and lows from month to month. If you only invest in the final month, then you might only experience a downward trend, which will not serve you or your money well. When you put your funds in early, you have a greater chance of catching those market highs that really expedite the process of financial growth.

If you take a look at the markets right now and then check on them again a week from now, there could be drastic changes that occur in between. Nothing is a guarantee when it comes to investing, but the markets are always going to keep moving, just as life keeps continuing onward. You can either choose to participate in this, or you can sit back and watch the markets while losing out on the potential investment opportunities that await. Many people are so closed-off to the investment world because they think it is complex or beyond their means. Based on what you've read so far, you can see that this isn't true. You can open a Roth IRA account and begin investing today if you truly want to.

One more benefit about investing early is getting to know more about the market highs and lows. You still have a lot to learn about their trends and how they operate. You need to figure out which markets are best for you and your investments. By doing this early on, you get more time to carefully consider the decisions that you make. If you only invest at the end of the contribution period, then you might feel rushed to make a decision. Being rushed to make any type of monetary decision usually doesn't lead to good results. You worked hard for this money, so you should treat it very valuably.

If you need someone to hold you accountable for making contributions and investing your money, confide in someone you trust. This can be your partner, a close friend, or even your financial advisor. When you speak about something that you plan on doing, it makes the plan seem so much more real. This will essentially give you the feeling of a fire being lit beneath you, causing you to take action. It's a great thing! We all need that push sometimes, and having an accountability buddy will remind you to stay on track with that great plan that you took the time to come up with.

Messing Up Your Budget

Imagine that you go the whole year without regularly contributing to your Roth IRA. This likely means that you aren't budgeting for it, otherwise, that money would be in the account already. If you attempt to go from not saving at all to suddenly putting a large sum of money into your Roth IRA account, this will very likely end up messing up your budget. When you don't plan for something from the start, you can't expect to financially support the idea if you decide to go forward with it at the last minute. You might even realize that you don't have any money left over to contribute to your Roth IRA if you wait too long, which results in an even worse feeling.

Having a Roth IRA account should make you feel confident and secure. This is your future, and you have a lot of control over it in this sense. Budgeting is not only a big part of your daily life but it also directly impacts your ability to save money. Many people factor in all of the money they need for necessities, even recreational purchases, but sometimes, it's easy to forget to set some aside for savings. If you are the type to see extra money and immediately want to spend it, then having a Roth IRA account is perfect for you because you can just put it into the account and pretend it doesn't exist. Even if you don't have this habit, it's still going to benefit you because you can essentially switch to auto-pilot as your money grows for you once it's invested.

This is a budget-making strategy that you can use that allows for both spending and saving. There must be a balance of the two if you want to have your necessities in life as well as your necessities for the future.

1. **Calculate your monthly income.** If you have one full-time job, this should be easy enough. You can simply take a look at your pay stubs or direct deposits. If you do anything else on the side that earns you money, don't forget to calculate that into your budget, as well.

2. **Make sure that the money you are counting as income is all after-tax money.** You wouldn't want to say that you make $3,000 monthly when you haven't considered how much of that money is going toward taxes or even an employer-provided 401(k) plan.

3. **Create a simple budgeting framework for yourself to follow**. This can be anything that works best for your lifestyle, but the 50/30/20 method is a popular one among many people. This method means that you spend 50% of your earned income on your needs—this includes things like bills, any repairs that you may need on your property, and so on. 30% then goes to your wants. This is what you can consider your spending money. The remaining 20% will then be put into savings.

4. **Keep track of your progress.** Having a plan and going through all of the proper steps is a great start! That's all it is, though—a start. You need to keep track of your progress to see if you're actually sticking to your budget. Everyone slips up sometimes, and unexpected expenses are always possible. Go easy on yourself if you have a bad budgeting week, but recognize that you can always quickly get back on track if you stick to the original plan.

5. **Consider automating your savings.** This means that you can assign a portion of your income to come out of your checking account and into your Roth IRA account automatically. Scheduling this in advance will prevent you from spending any money that you don't wish to spend. It also protects you from the possibility of forgetting to save up

for the month. Automation is typically a huge help for those who want to become better at saving.

With these tools, you should be able to create a budget, make a plan, and stick with it. Times might get tough during the year, but you have all of the knowledge you need to understand why it is crucial to begin investing your Roth IRA contributions as early as possible. Don't wait until you only have days left!

7

THE POWER OF ROTH CONVERSIONS

As discussed briefly in a prior chapter, a Roth IRA conversion applies to the idea that you can take funds from a different retirement account and put them into your Roth IRA account. It is essentially a money transfer. As you read on, you will find out why some people do this and what the benefits are to doing this. You may already have another retirement account in place, in which case, this information will highly benefit you to learn more about. There is a lot of power behind Roth conversions simply because a lot of people don't know about them.

Once you understand all of the rules and how to make the transfers properly, you might be able to grow your wealth even more than you originally imagined. A Roth conversion is yet another tool to add to your ever-growing list of knowledge. There is nothing too complicated or stressful about it, so you can be sure that you aren't making any mistakes if you do decide to go down this route. This is also a topic that is often discussed with financial advisors when individuals don't know what to do with their external accounts.

How It Works

You can think about a conversion as a rollover plan for your funds. This is similar to what a lot of cell phone companies offer. If you leave your money in a tax-deferred account such as a 401(k), you will have to pay whatever your income tax rate is at the time you withdraw money for retirement. However, when you use the conversion method, you are able to roll this money into your Roth IRA account, and then pay lower income taxes for the year at your current tax bracket.

It's very likely that your tax bracket will change as you age. By most standards, those who are older and who are more experienced hold better jobs—this also means higher salaries. The more money you make, the more taxes you have to pay. This is why your tax bracket matters so much during your estimated retirement age. Once you convert your retirement account into your Roth IRA account, you will be paying taxes on the money, but it is going to be at a lower rate right now. This benefits you in the future because you will be able to collect the money tax-free by the time you reach your retirement age.

Above all, conversions are another investment strategy. You don't need to convert anything you do not feel comfortable with, but it's encouraged if you feel that you can pay more taxes now to save money in the future. It makes sense for most people to do this because nobody likes being met with fees at the end of a very long process. You are going to want your nest egg, and you are going to want to be able to access it easily. If you have a lot of taxes to pay on this money by the time you reach retirement, this could even deter you from retiring when you want to because of the taxes due.

This is a lot to think about, but the younger you are, the more it's encouraged to pursue. If you already have a 401(k) plan set up with your full-time job, think about converting this into your Roth IRA account. Not only will you have the tax advantages mentioned above, but you will also have more freedom with the way that you invest your money as opposed to your employer controlling where and how your money is invested. The downside is that before you convert your 401(k) into your Roth IRA, you need to pay income taxes on it so that the money becomes after-tax dollars. This is something that you'll definitely have to think about before making any conversions.

It isn't only 401(k) plans that you receive at work that are able to be converted into Roth IRA accounts. You can also convert traditional IRAs, simplified employee pension plans, and simple IRAs (given to employees by small businesses). Keeping this factor in mind, it's safe to assume that almost any other retirement account you have in place right now can possibly be converted to your Roth IRA account. Many people don't know about this because it isn't usually something mentioned to those who are just starting out with Roth IRA accounts.

This is a slightly more advanced investment strategy, but this book is meant to give you as many options and ideas as possible. You need to be prepared for your future, and that includes taking whatever measures you feel that you must take to secure your nest egg. You already know all of the great advantages of having a Roth

IRA account, so why not add more funds to it from other accounts that you may already have in place? It seems like a no-brainer because it is. The actual process isn't as simple as clicking a button, but with the help of a financial advisor, it's possible to move this money around. All you have to do is bring up the idea, then they will tell you their thoughts on why you should or should not go for the conversion.

Who Do Conversions Apply To?

A conversion may apply to you if you are a career-oriented person. This is the case because you'll be working hard to advance your career over the next few decades. In this time, you are sure to get better-paying jobs, which will boost you into higher tax brackets. As mentioned, this is why you might end up paying taxes on your tax-deferred contributions by the time you reach retirement age. If you know that you are probably on your current lifelong career path and you want to move forward with it, then conversions would make sense for you.

You might also be expecting a big promotion in your near future. If this is the case and you already know you are going to be moving into a different tax bracket early on, then a conversion would benefit you. Any time that you can anticipate making more money than you do right now, you can likely assume that this is going to change the way that you pay your taxes at the end of each fiscal year.

Essentially, a Roth IRA conversion can apply to anyone at any time. It's a personal decision for you to make, and it can become one of the smartest you will make with your investments. The main point is that you take into consideration the amount of taxes that are going to be due at the end of each fiscal year. If you are in a lower tax bracket already accounting for this, then you shouldn't have a problem paying slightly more in taxes now to be tax-free when you withdraw your money from your Roth IRA in the future. Conversions are all about perspective, and you need to take the time to consider if it's the right financial move for you.

Another case when a conversion could apply is when you lose your job. If you have an employer-provided 401(k) plan, you will naturally no longer have this plan once you stop working at that place of employment. To protect the investments you have already made, you'll need to quickly move your money to safety. Your Roth IRA can become this safety net, and it can catch all of the funds that you have accumulated while you were working at that job. Nobody ever plans to get fired or laid off, but these are things that happen commonly in life. It's always a good idea to have a backup plan.

If taxes are of no concern to you, at the very least, a Roth IRA conversion can simplify your financial situation. When you have multiple accounts open with multiple banks, this can get confusing. You already have a full and busy life, so why complicate things even more with your money? Each cent should be accounted for, and converting your other retirement accounts into your Roth IRA account can serve as a swift solution to this problem. Since everything will be in one place, under one investment portfolio, you'll never spread yourself thin trying to remember where all of your funds are located.

Most younger people do not mind having their money in multiple banks or with several establishments, but the older you get, the more complex life can become. You might find that as you mature, you'll wish to simplify your financial situation, and then you can make the conversion. The great thing is that there is no deadline to miss out on. If you decide you want to make a Roth IRA conversion, all you have to do is inform your current Roth IRA establishment/your financial advisor. They will help you complete this process.

Just because you don't fit certain financial molds does not mean you should not apply for a conversion if you feel that it's what is best for your money. Since this decision is based on both logic and personal preference, you do have the ability to make a Roth IRA conversion simply because you feel it's what is right for your life. The more that you handle your money and attempt to become better at managing it, the easier it will be to make these decisions that once seemed so foreign. Roth IRA conversions are not scary or dangerous processes; they are actually pretty simple if you think about it.

Advantages and Disadvantages of Conversions

Now that you know more about conversions, you probably have a lot of thinking to do. While weighing your options, you should always know both the advantages and disadvantages of each option. This book is not meant to sway you in any one direction. Its purpose is to guide you toward the knowledge you need to perform your due diligence. You get to decide what to do and if you are going to do it, especially when it comes to matters that concern moving your money around. Consider the following pros and cons of each option before you make your final decision. Seeing them in a comparative light can be both useful and enlightening.

Advantages

You can be sure to tax advantage of tax-free withdrawals once you reach retirement age. It's a great feeling to know that you have this sum of money simply waiting for you until you are ready to use it, and since it has already been taxed, you have nothing else to worry about! This is a big reason why many do Roth IRA conversions in their lifetimes.

If your money is in a traditional IRA, you are forced to take the required minimum distributions each year (RMDs) after you reach 72. Or, after you reach 70 ½ if you opened the account before the current year. This happens regardless of whether or not you need the money. So essentially, you are unable to keep those funds in the account to maintain that tax-free growth that is so beneficial with the Roth IRA. When you have a Roth IRA, there are no RMDs. This gives you an advantage when you make a Roth IRA conversion because you won't have to worry about any required RMDs, meaning you will have more freedom.

Thinking about what happens after retirement, you never know where life will take you. There will likely be some loved ones that you'd like to leave your money to after you pass away. With a Roth IRA, this is possible because you are providing an inheritance for your loved ones without providing any extra debt. Since the beginning, your debts were already paid. There is already a lot to worry about when it comes to managing the finances of someone who has passed away, but this option gives your loved ones guidance and a simple plan of what to do next.

With a Roth IRA conversion, your money is all in one place and growing under the same terms and conditions. This is important for many, as mentioned, because of the busy lives and stressors that already exist. When you have a family, a job, a social life, and your personal well-being to consider, it may not be helpful to have multiple retirement accounts that all have different rules. You can simplify your life with a Roth IRA conversion, and it will feel great knowing that your money is all growing tax-free depending on how you invest it.

If you decide that you can retire early, a Roth IRA conversion will work to your advantage because that means there will be more of a nest egg for you to rely on. Without this conversion, the money may have been in a prior account that was untouchable. Retiring early isn't always an option with retirement accounts that set very particular withdrawal rules in place. However, you can leverage other retirement accounts and roll the money over into your Roth IRA to take advantage of its flexible rules around withdrawals. Using a Roth IRA can open doors for more financial freedom while growing your wealth.

Disadvantages

Since it is possible to make multiple and large conversions, these instances could push you into a higher tax bracket. While you won't have to pay taxes on the money that already exists in your Roth IRA account, being in a higher tax bracket impacts every other part of your life in which you do still owe taxes. This is something to consider, and it definitely depends on how much money you have in other accounts. If you plan on doing a conversion, be smart about it. Double-check to see which tax bracket you will remain in post-conversion.

In an earlier chapter, you learned that you have to actually make the same amount in earned income as the amount you contribute to your Roth IRA account. For example, if you made the maximum annual contribution of $6,000, you would have to have this much in actual earned money. The same is true with conversions. You need to have the liquid assets to cover this conversion, and this typically becomes a problem when you try to process large ones. If you don't have the liquid assets, you may have a withholding tax placed on your converted balance—just another reason to be extra careful about how much money you do convert.

You can withdraw your contributions and conversions at any time from your Roth IRA account, but the same is not true with investment earnings. Naturally, when you make a Roth IRA conversion, this gives you more money to invest with. The more you invest, the more possible return. With investment earnings, you are subject to a five-year waiting period if you want to withdraw any of these funds. This shouldn't be a problem for most who truly want to use their Roth IRAs as retirement accounts, but this could pose an issue for early retirement or for Roth IRAs being treated as emergency savings.

Backdoor Roth IRA & Mega Backdoor Roth IRA

Backdoor Roth IRA

From an earlier chapter, you have become somewhat familiar with backdoor Roth IRAs—a method that allows higher-income individuals to make additional contributions to their accounts even though they were only eligible for partial to no contribution. Put simply, if you only qualify for a partial contribution or are not eligible at all, this is a legal loophole that allows you to bypass contribution limits by moving your money through different accounts so that you can max out your Roth IRA. Now, let's put two concepts together—conversions and backdoor Roth IRAs. Conversions make the backdoor Roth possible. Before you do anything, make sure you understand the rules.

Rules

There may be consequences for not properly following conversion rules. There are two main ones that you must consider:

1. The "Same Trustee Transfer" Rule
2. The Pro-Rata Rule

Same Trustee Transfer

The "same trustee transfer" rule means that the conversion needs to be a rollover, meaning that *you* need to have this money in another account in order to put it into *your* account. If someone else were to try to put their money into your Roth IRA account, this is still possible (spouses do this all the time), but this does not quite fall under the category of a Roth IRA conversion. It is essentially saying that you are giving yourself this money.

What this rule also means is that you cannot simply take a liquid savings account and roll it over into a Roth IRA conversion—that is considered a normal contribution. You need to have another retirement account in place, whether it be independently or through your job. This is what is necessary to make a proper Roth IRA conversion, and this is how the "backdoor" method works out which allows you to go over your maximum annual contribution limit.

Pro-Rata Rule

Another rule to consider is the pro-rata rule. You already know that the money you originally contributed to your Roth IRA is made with after-tax funds, and the IRS knows this, too. However, when you convert, you are contributing a portion of the money that is pre-taxed. This means that the IRS will have to do a calculation to determine how much you owe on this pre-tax money. To get these figures, they use a calculation that takes the total after-tax amount in all IRA accounts that you own, and then it divides them by the total value of all IRA accounts. With this figure, they then multiply the amount that you converted.

Here is a working example of the pro-rata rule: Imagine that you have contributed three $5,000 non-deductible contributions to an IRA over the past couple of years. This makes for a $15,000 total. The Roth IRA is now worth $20,000 because of investment growth. With your rollover account that is worth $80,000, you convert $20,000 of this money into your Roth IRA. When this happens, $3,000 will be considered after-tax and $17,000 will be considered pre-tax. This is the formula in action: $15,000 divided by $100,000 = 15%; $20,000 x 15% = 3,000.

Mega Backdoor Roth IRA

In short, the mega backdoor Roth IRA conversion allowed people to contribute up to $37,500 in their Roth IRA or Roth 401(k) in 2020— on top of their $6,000 base contribution! Instead of compounding interest on a measly $6,000 alone, you can see why a mega backdoor would be appealing. This may be a great option for those who have already maxed out their 401(k) and Roth IRA, yet still have money lying around to save or invest. You may be wondering; how does it work? To better understand if this conversion is suited for you, you must understand both the risks and rewards involved. This is a caveat, which means it serves as yet another way to put even more money into your Roth IRA account. To create a mega backdoor Roth IRA, you must have the following in place:

1. **You need an existing 401(k)** plan that allows "after-tax contributions." According to a 2017 survey, Willis Towers Watson consulting firm stated that around 43% of employer-provided 401(k) plans have this feature (Coombes, 2020).

2. **Your employer must offer in-service distributions**, which means you can take money out of your 401(k) while you are still working at the company. Alternatively, they must allow you to move some of your after-tax money into the Roth. If you are unsure about these terms, it's important to talk to someone at your company about them.

3. **Finally, you need to have this extra money to save**. It seems like a no-brainer but consider the contribution limits. If you've already met your Roth IRA limit and your 401(k) limit with money left over, this is going to offer you a great strategy to maximize your money even more.

If you are still confused as to whether or not you qualify for a mega backdoor Roth IRA strategy, you can search online for calculators that allow you to input your real figures. This will help you see on paper whether or not it's a smart financial move to make.

The pros and cons are very similar to the backdoor Roth IRA method. You still have to be careful that you aren't pushing yourself into a higher tax bracket while doing this, and you also have to consider that you are going to be paying taxes upfront rather than in the future. If you are willing to do this to ultimately have a completely tax-free experience when you need to withdraw your money at retirement age or give it as an inheritance, then a mega backdoor Roth IRA might be great for you.

This is a more complex strategy that should definitely be discussed with a professional before you begin, but having this information now gives you an idea of what the strategy is and how it could potentially benefit you and your finances. It's always wonderful to see that there are many options you've probably never even heard about or thought about that you can take on your financial journey.

Timing is Key

You can still make a plan that will allow you to reduce the taxes you'll have to pay on the money that you roll over. This is why timing is key when it comes to conversions. Consider these helpful tips for timing a conversion if you plan on making one. They will help you not only lessen the financial burden but also the potential stress involved.

1. **Lower Tax Brackets:** If you find yourself in a lower tax bracket for any reason, this is a good time to plan on doing a conversion. The rates will be lower, and this will make it easier for you as you move your money around. There are several reasons why you might enter a lower tax bracket,

from changing jobs to even losing a job. Why not take advantage of this situation?

2. **Traditional Balance Down:** If you have a traditional IRA account in place, consider making a conversion if the market takes a hit. This will cause your account to feel an aftershock, so getting some of that money out of there and into the protection of a Roth IRA is a smart financial move to make.

3. **Early in Tax Year:** Since Tax Day is on April 15, you should always keep in mind when you are attempting to make your conversions. The earlier in the tax year, the better—this is simply because you'll have more time to pay your taxes. If you make the conversion right before Tax Day, then you are going to be hit with a lot of taxes that you probably weren't accounting for throughout the year. Start as early as you can if you have the funding to do so.

4. **A Little at a Time:** Understand that you don't have to convert your entire balance all at once! You can convert your money in small increments that are easy to manage and to keep track of. This also prevents you from having to pay a huge amount in taxes at the end of the year. While you should be living within your means, this concept also applies to the way that you go about making your Roth IRA conversions.

These are just a couple of strategies and pieces of advice to keep in mind as you consider making a Roth IRA conversion. They are meant to guide you, but by no means do you have to fully commit to one or the other. In fact, you don't have to make any conversions at all if you don't feel comfortable with the idea! Getting to know more about how it works is the first step to fully understanding if the process is going to be personally beneficial to you.

At the end of the day, this is your future and your money. You need to make whatever financial decisions you feel will work best for the current plan that you have. And while plans can change, the option to convert will always be available for you to take. You should especially consider the timing of any conversions that you decide to make if you plan on retiring early or if you think that it could be an option. Because of the five-year rule involved and the tax bracket you may be in at the time of early retirement, you need to carefully consider if this is the smartest move for you to make for your future. This topic will be discussed in-depth in the following chapter, providing you with even more insights to consider.

8

WITHDRAWING FROM YOUR ROTH IRA

Withdrawing from your account is a topic of interest that has probably been on your mind since you began reading this book. With most retirement accounts, you are not allowed to make withdrawals without jumping through hoops, but this is where your Roth IRA sets you apart—you can withdraw your money at any time! Of course, just because you can doesn't mean you should. There are still a few rules that indirectly apply to your withdrawal method, and your ultimate end goal should always be taken into consideration before you take any money out of the account.

This chapter is going to break down some important information that you need to know about making withdrawals. Whether you plan on retiring early or you need some emergency funds, all of this information will be valuable for you to know. There are a few different ways that you can withdraw from your account, and this chapter will cover them in detail so that there aren't any questions left unanswered. Clarity is most important when dealing with your finances!

The Five-Year Rule

You may recall the term "five-year rule" mentioned a couple of times now throughout this book. This is something that you should consider, but it is not complicated or detrimental to your desire to withdraw your money. What this rule entails is that you must wait for a certain amount of time until your interest earned is considered tax-free. This interest earned can come in the form of your investments, such as returns on stocks or mutual funds that you decided to invest in when you first opened your Roth IRA account. The contributions that you make and the conversions that you make do not fall under this five-year rule, only the interest that you have earned.

There are two simple things to remember if you want to know if you can fully withdraw tax-free:

- You must be 59 ½
- You must have waited five tax years since making your first contribution

If either one of these applies to you, then you should be able to withdraw your money, interest earnings included, tax-free—it's that simple! Many people feel overwhelmed when they hear about this rule because five years seems like a long time. In a sense, it is a long time, but it's simply a safeguard that is applied to your account by the establishment that you bank with. Most people don't have to worry much about the five-year rule because they typically don't drain the entire account in one go. This has a lot of risks attached because of the higher tax bracket issue, as discussed in the prior chapter.

The clock starts the instant that you make your first contribution to your Roth IRA account. Even if you open the account and only put in $20, this still gets the five-year clock ticking. As a young person, this is important to remember. You don't need to make a huge contribution right away to start receiving the benefits of a Roth IRA account—the sooner the better! If you only have a little bit to contribute right now, that's nothing to feel ashamed of. You can do what you can until you have a solid financial plan in place. What matters most is that you are actively working toward a goal.

Something else you should consider is the conversions that you make. If you do decide to roll over some funds from a separate account into your Roth IRA account, then your five-year clock does not reset. It starts from the very beginning, as mentioned when you make your first contribution. Nothing will "stop the clock," so to speak, or reset it. This is a nice thing to realize because you can confidently make conversions without having to worry that your original contributions will be stuck because of them.

The Second Part of the Five-Year Rule

There is a second part to the five-year rule, but it is also very simple to understand and should not impact you very much in a negative way. This rule only applies if you have decided to make any conversions. This rule is solely designed to determine if the distribution of principal from this conversion qualifies as penalty-free money or not. If you do not plan on making any conversions or if you do not plan on withdrawing any of the money that you have converted, then this rule will not apply to you. Still, it helps to understand it in case either situation arises.

When you make a contribution that comes from conversion, the same five-year rule above will apply to it. However, the main difference is that the conversion must be made by December 31st. This is different from typical Roth IRA contributions because it's operating based on the calendar year rather than the tax year. Again, this is something you probably won't have to think about too much, as most people do not typically drain their entire retirement accounts in one go, regardless of how the money was contributed or how much the money has grown.

Taking a conversion example into consideration, say you converted your traditional IRA into your Roth IRA in November of 2019. This means that your five-year waiting period begins on January 1st, 2019. Say you did the same thing, but you did it in February of 2020. This would mean that your five-year waiting period would begin on January 1st, 2020. It has already been stressed, but this is why timing is so important when it comes to conversions and to Roth IRA contributions of any kind. You need to make sure that it makes sense on your given timeline.

Keep in mind that each conversion you make, no matter how large or how small is going to have its own five-year waiting period. This means that the $100 conversion you made in 2020 is going to have a different five-year period than the $1,000 conversion you potentially make in 2022. In this case, it can be hard to keep track of which conversions have which waiting periods. Most financial advisors would recommend that you make regular conversions if you plan on starting out small. This way, it is on a schedule and is less confusing to keep track of.

If you make many random conversions throughout the year without keeping track of how much you roll over and when, it's very easy to forget when you are technically allowed to withdraw your interest earnings. Keep things simple for yourself by planning out any conversions you want to make. You can either do this on your own or with the help of a financial advisor. When you schedule a conversion regularly, like an appointment, you will have an easier time remembering what is going on with your money.

In general, it's also a great idea to get into the habit of scheduling any kind of financial transactions because consistency is important if you'd like to see financial gain. You need to turn this into a good habit that you keep up with if you want your nest egg to continue growing. Even with the five-year rule, this is entirely possible with smart planning and a little research.

Qualified Distributions

There are exceptions to the five-year rule called qualified distributions, which allow you to avoid the 10% penalty and taxes. To be eligible for a qualified contribution, you still need to be at least 59½ years old and wait five years from your first contribution and then some:

1. **If you die** before the five-year time period has elapsed, then your beneficiary will be allowed access to the funds. Your beneficiary will be able to withdraw everything from the account, no matter if it's principal or earnings despite the

rule. It is unfortunate to consider, but it is a realistic possibility

2. **If you have a permanent disability** and aren't able to work, you may withdraw money for expenses and use it for anything you'd like.

3. **If you are planning on buying your first home**, then you are allowed to use up to $10,000 to pay your down payment, even if you have yet to meet the five-year mark.

4. **If you are paying for a higher education.** You can use the same amount of money to pay for college expenses for yourself, your spouse, your children, or your grandchildren. Age and length of time both do not matter in this case.

5. **If it's going toward childbirth or adoption,** you may withdraw funds from your Roth IRA account to help pay for childbirth costs or adoption fees. The limit is $5,000, and the withdrawal must be made within one year of the event. There is a little more lenience here because it is understandable that childbirth and adoption can both be unpredictable life events.

6. **If you are paying for unreimbursed medical expenses.** This basically means that any medical expenses that you had to pay out-of-pocket when you had health insurance might be considered non-qualified distributions. If the total of these expenses exceeds 10% of your adjusted gross income, then you can look into this option for yourself to help you pay off the bills. The 10% formula applies to the AGI (adjusted gross income) of the current year that you are trying to withdraw the funds.

7. **If you're paying for medical insurance.** If you lost your job that included medical insurance, then you have lost two very valuable necessities. This is considered a non-qualified distribution, and it is a special circumstance to consider if you are in a tough spot because of the back-to-back losses.

8. **If you're withdrawing substantially equal periodic payments.** If you withdraw the same amount every year for five years until the day you turn 59 ½, you may do so penalty free.

9. **If you fulfill an IRS levy,** meaning you have unpaid federal taxes, then the IRS can bill your Roth IRA. However, you cannot withdraw it yourself. The IRS must withdraw it directly from your account.

One other instance of an exception is when the IRS allows you to withdraw funds to pay for health insurance premiums. You do not have to obey the five-year rule if you have to pay for your health insurance and become unemployed. Also, you may withdraw from your Roth IRA before five years if you have any outstanding medical bills that account for over 10% of your adjusted gross income.

The benefit of a qualified distribution is that it will not be included in your gross income, which frees you from owing taxes or penalties on the withdrawals.

Non-Qualified Distributions

A non-qualified distribution are withdrawals that are suject to taxes and a 10% penalty. This is anything that doesn't meet the exceptions and requirements stated above. Be prepared for any consequences if you do decide to take out a non-qualified distribution. Choose wisely.

Withdrawal Hacking for Early Retirement

This concept almost sounds like a dangerous one, but withdrawal hacking is simply a strategy used by those who plan on retiring early. Even if the early retirement is unplanned, it can still come in handy to know all about withdrawal hacking in case the opportunity to retire early becomes available to you. This "hack" essentially revolves around you tapping into your Roth IRA account before you reach the age of 59 ½. It gives you more financial freedom than the exceptions already mentioned above, especially if you don't qualify for them.

The Roth IRA Conversion Ladder

To apply this hack and to retire early with your funds in-hand, you can use the method known as the conversion ladder. Much like you'd imagine, this method involves working your way up the rungs of a ladder in a sense.

1. **Invest in your employer's pre-tax retirement accounts**. If you have any pre-tax retirement accounts to contribute to, you'll want to go ahead and do so. This includes traditional IRAs and 401(k) plans. The money that you put into these decrease the amount of taxes you'll have to pay and should be contributed while you have a career.

2. **The next step is the best of all—retire early!** It seems like a big jump, but this is only the second rung of the ladder.

After this, you'll want to transfer your employer's retirement account(s), such as the 401(k), to your traditional IRA account.

3. **Then, perform a Backdoor Roth conversion.** You'll convert your traditional IRA to your Roth IRA. Remember that you will have to pay taxes upfront on this conversion, so make it wisely. You don't have to go for the lump sum all at once. If you need to make a few conversions, plan this out.

4. **Next, wait five years** until you touch the converted money! This ensures that you are following the five-year rule, but you will also still be set for your early retirement. In the meantime, you can still withdraw from the non-converted funds in your Roth IRA account if you need money to get by. After the five-year period is over, you can withdraw the conversions tax-free and penalty-free! At the end of this, you'll have extra money to use during your early retirement.

Further Details

The above was a simplified method of this concept of withdrawal hacking, but there are still a few finer details that you need to understand if you want to pursue this strategy. When you realize that you want to retire early, set this as a goal in your mind. You must pick an age to give you an idea of the timeline that you are going to be working with. It takes a lot of thought and there are many factors involved, but this is a personal decision to make as the very first step of your withdrawal hacking plan. Once you have an age in mind, then you can move forward with the planning stage.

For example, if you are 30 years old and your living expenses are about $40,000 a year, you need to have about $1,000,000 saved up for retirement to last you for another 30 years. Mind that most people who follow this method also have passive income streams besides retirement accounts that can provide cashflow.

From there, you must pick an estimated date for when you'll quit your job. You will also need to make sure you open a traditional IRA account, so if you don't have one already you will have to open one quickly online to perform a Backdoor Roth IRA conversion.

Each time you roll over money from your traditional IRA account into your Roth IRA account, you will have to pay taxes on it. However, you'll likely be in a lower tax bracket since you've quit your job, making the taxes quite manageable. That said, you'll still need to take taxes into account when deciding when and how much money to convert.

Of course, the waiting period is pretty self-explanatory. You must wait five years until you can have access to this converted money. The five years ensure that your money becomes non-taxable. If you have made several conversions, plan this out carefully and set reminders, so you can keep your income stream flowing in order for it to carry you through the first part of your early retirement. A study done on historical stock and bond market returns since 1926 revealed that the optimal rate of withdrawal in retirement is 4%. The 4% rule ensures that you will have enough money to sustain your withdrawals to where you won't have too much money leftover or zero money at all.

You will likely need to repeat the above steps more than once throughout your early retirement. If necessary, repeat the steps each year until your money is completely withdrawn. Essentially, this is what withdrawal hacking entails, and many people have been using this strategy for many years already. With the desire to retire early becoming a more popular option in today's society, this is a very important strategy to learn in case you end up following along on the same path. If you are interested, definitely look into the F.I.R.E. movement, which stands for "financially independent, retire early."

Examples

When individuals decide on how much money to withdraw, they usually look back on their annual expenses for past years. Of course, there should be some sort of cushion included in case of emergencies or unexpected expenses, but you can easily figure out how much money you need to roll over if you take a look at your prior spending habits. While reading all of these steps can seem like a lot to go through, it may be easier for some to visualize this using a real-life example. Taking Jade's decision to retire early, you can learn a lot from what she went through and how she got from point A to point B.

Jade Plans Ahead

Jade, a 35-year-old insurance agent, decided that she didn't want to wait until she turned 60 to retire. A lot of her friends started talking about early retirement, and she never thought it would be possible for her. This idea got her thinking, though. Jade began to explore her options, and this is when she came across an article on the internet about withdrawal hacking. At first, she was skeptical. It sounded like something that she shouldn't be doing, but then she realized that it's simply a strategy for those who want to retire early—just like her friends.

At only 25-years-old, Jade got her insurance license and quickly worked her way up the corporate ladder at her agency. From junior agent to senior account manager, Jade knew that this was the career path she was planning on sticking with. With a salary that pays well, an employer-provided 401(k) plan, and awesome coworkers to pass the time with, she felt content about her career and how she made it to this point. Even though everything in Jade's career was going well, she still had a curiosity about early retirement and if she would ever qualify for it.

Her job paid well from the start, and after being there for a decade so far, she obtained quite a few pay raises. The income she was making was substantial enough to last her for a few years, but she was still doubtful that it would carry her all the way through to an early retirement plan that would be permanent. The last thing Jade wanted was to give up this great job and to have to reemerge in the workforce after a failed attempt at early retirement. She has always been a thorough planner, so this case was no exception for her—Jade began to brainstorm.

While she enjoyed working at the insurance agency very much, she wondered if she could potentially retire after 10 more years. This would put her at 45-years-old, much younger than she originally thought she would retire because she had no idea that early retirement might even be an option. Looking back at her past expenses, she ended up realizing that she needs around $50,000 a year to survive. This includes her expenses, her recreational purchases, and some savings for emergencies. Since she recognized this pattern, she started looking into options of how to use backdoor IRAs, conversions, and this withdrawal hacking method. In preparation for early retirement, she decided to roll over $50,000 by the time she turned 40-years-old. This would make her five-year waiting period coincide perfectly with her desired early retirement age of 45.

During this time, she continued working hard and taking on as many clients as she could. This income that she was still earning was a crucial part of her early retirement plan because it was the income that was going to sustain her until she ultimately left her job. Scheduling regular conversions, she was able to successfully retire at age 45 and have a comfortable life. She didn't have to worry about being able to pay her bills or cover her other expenses, and this is all thanks to Jade learning about withdrawal hacking. She was able to maximize her investments in a way that allowed her to see her plan through to the end.

Pros and Cons of Withdrawal Hacking

While there are many reasons why people may want to pursue withdrawal hacking, the reason that makes the most logical sense is because of an early retirement plan. If you already know you don't want to do this or can't realistically do this, then withdrawal hacking probably isn't going to come into play in your financial strategy. That's okay! Not everyone retires early, but that still doesn't negate the fact that having options and having a Roth IRA account in place is still setting you up for the best future possible.

Since there are always advantages and disadvantages to every decision, it's time to take a look at the pros and cons of withdrawal hacking. Assuming that this is something you want to move forward with, taking a look at them together will give you a better idea if this is something you can realistically afford to do. The answer may surprise you, so you shouldn't rule the option out just because you can't see it happening right now. These pros and cons of withdrawal hacking take into account both your present and your future. Carefully consider each option as you move forward with your plan.

Pros

- With withdrawal hacking, this provides you a plan where you can retire early!
- When timed correctly, it's easy to figure out how to successfully plan for your future and have enough money to live off of after quitting your job.
- The earlier you start with your retirement accounts, the more set you will be for your future, even during an early retirement scenario.
- Withdrawal hacking is a completely legal way to maximize your money and earnings.
- There are many tips and strategies that you can follow if you want to retire early, so you'll never have to go through any part of it unguided.

Cons

- You must have multiple retirement accounts open to successfully complete the process of withdrawal hacking to retire early. If you don't, then opening a backdoor IRA is probably a step you'll have to take.
- You need to calculate exactly how much money you'll need to live off of if you want to retire early, and this can require tedious number-crunching when you decide to do this on your own.
- This is a continuous process that you'll probably have to repeat annually until you are able to withdraw all of your money and earnings from your Roth IRA account.
- It becomes easy to accidentally roll over too much money, putting you into a higher tax bracket. This is another aspect where you'll have to make sure you have great attention to detail.

Comparing all of these pros and cons, you should be able to decide if early retirement is the right step for your career. With withdrawal hacking, you can see that it is definitely possible, and it's probably a lot easier than you imagined! Always be cautious once you begin the process because it's likely you'll need help from a financial advisor at first. However, this isn't a negative thing—everyone needs guidance at some point.

9

PASSING DOWN YOUR ROTH TO A BENEFICIARY

We've talked a lot about what you can personally do with your Roth IRA account and how to use it, but what will happen to the leftover money once you pass away? Assuming you do still have money in your Roth IRA account after you die, you have the option to leave this money to a beneficiary. Many people list their spouses, children, or grandchildren as beneficiaries. This inheritance of money is important for many reasons, and when planned correctly, it can set your beneficiary up for a very positive future ahead.

When you first open your Roth IRA account, you are given the option to list a beneficiary. This may seem unimportant at the time, and you may even bypass the option if you are opening your account while you are still fairly young. The truth is, you never know what could happen in life. Since our days are not guaranteed, selecting a beneficiary for your account is a way to provide your loved one with a nest egg that they can access without any rules or penalties.

Even if you don't want to think about what will happen to your account after you die, it's still important to list a beneficiary regardless of your age right now. Without a beneficiary, this money will likely become part of your estate, which is then determined by who you list in your will. It's also pretty common that if you don't list a beneficiary that you also don't have a will—this isn't something that the younger generation tends to think about because of their age, but things become complex with your estate if you don't determine who you are leaving what to.

Your beneficiary can be anybody that you want, and you can change it at any time. If you are currently unmarried and without children, this decision might be difficult for you. Remember that you can pick a friend to be your beneficiary or you could pick another important influence in your life, like a cousin or other family member. If you do end up getting married in the future, you always have the option to change the beneficiary to your spouse or children. No matter how weird it feels right now, it's a smart action to take when you open your Roth IRA account. Make sure that you have one listed to avoid any complexities after you pass away.

Having a beneficiary on the account makes it clear to the bank who gets to be in charge of the Roth IRA account after you're gone. This person will be informed of their new inheritance, and they will get an explanation of how they can withdraw these funds and what needs to happen next. If you are worried about your beneficiary getting stuck with any taxes or fees, just remember that your contributions are already made with after-tax earnings. You will not be transferring any debt onto your beneficiary by leaving them your Roth IRA account, regardless of how much money happens to be in it at the time.

Planning: Why it Matters

When you sign up for your Roth IRA account, you will be asked to submit basic information about yourself first. Then, there will be a section that asks you to list your beneficiary. Before opening the account, you should have someone in mind whom you'd like to list. Because this can be changed in the future, you shouldn't stress yourself out over who you pick right now. This person may stay your beneficiary for the entire length of you having the Roth IRA account or it may change as your life changes. The Roth IRA is truly a transformative retirement option that makes for great and easy estate-planning.

These are some scenarios that detail what will happen when you select certain beneficiaries. Better understanding the process will reiterate just how important it is to select a beneficiary. Without one listed on the account, the money may end up in the wrong hands and important tax benefits will be lost.

Spousal Inheritance

If you list your spouse as your beneficiary, there are four options that they can choose from according to what they wish to do with the money. Of course, all of these options vary greatly because you don't know how old your spouse will be when they inherit your

Roth IRA account, and you never know what they may wish to do with the funds at that time.

Spousal Transfer

When a spousal transfer happens, the spouse is now essentially the owner of the Roth IRA account. They treat it as their own. This means that they'll be subject to the same rules that you were subject to when it comes to making contributions and withdrawals. This is a method that might be sought if your spouse wishes to keep growing the account for the rest of their future, maybe even for the future of your children. To complete this transfer, your spouse will either have the funds transferred into their own existing Roth IRA account or they'll open one.

There are some things to take into consideration with this method. Since your spouse will be subject to the same Roth IRA account rules that you were, they will be able to withdraw contributions at any time, but they'll still have to abide by the five-year rule to withdraw earnings until they reach age 59 ½. Keep in mind that these earnings are taxable. The good news about the five-year rule, in this case, is that it applies to when you first contributed to the account, not five years from when your spouse inherits it.

This freedom is only going to be open to your spouse if they are the sole beneficiary, meaning if they are the only one. Some people can select more than one beneficiary, but that does tend to complicate matters because methods like this become impossible. Once your spouse has completed the transfer, they can then select their own beneficiary. It's almost like a pay-it-forward type of inheritance.

Open an Inherited IRA, Life Expectancy Method

Selecting this option means that your beneficiary will move the funds into what is known as an inherited Roth IRA. It will be in your name, but it will be a different account since it's now owned by your beneficiary. With the life expectancy method, it is exactly how it sounds—the inherited account is going to require the beneficiary to take required minimum distributions based on their given life expectancy. There is the option to postpone these distributions until the date the original account holder would've turned 72 or until December 31st of the year following the death of the original account holder.

Because the distributions are spread over your beneficiary's life expectancy, they should not be very large amounts of money. Usually, it's fairly easy to maintain these distributions without many additional financial hardships. If there are other beneficiaries listed, the life expectancy method will operate based on the life expectancy of the oldest individual. This is when things may get complicated for those who are younger beneficiaries. Your beneficiaries can avoid this complexity by opening separate inherited IRA accounts, as long as they do so before December 31st of the year following the year of the original account holder's death.

With this method, beneficiaries can still withdraw contributions at any time. The earnings are still going to be subject to the five-year rule, just the same as the above method mentioned. There will be no 10% early-withdrawal penalty, and assets that are in the account will continue to grow tax-free. Finally, the inherited account owner(s) also get to choose their own beneficiary(s).

Open an Inherited IRA, Five-Year Method

Like the name implies, this method centers around the five-year rule but a different one. This five-year rule revolves around how long the beneficiary has to transfer all of the funds from the original account into the inherited account. They do have the option to spread out the required distributions, which are also necessary with this method, but all of the money needs to be out of the original account by December 31st of the fifth year following the year that the original account holder passed away. This does give the beneficiary plenty of time to make those required distributions, and it takes away a little bit of the pressure.

Still, with this method, contributions can be withdrawn at any time. The earnings are taxable unless the original five-year rule is met, but there is a good chance that it will already be met by the time the original account holder passes away. Of course, there are certain circumstances where someone will pass away young and unexpectedly, therefore, causing the beneficiary to remain in the waiting period for a little longer. The beneficiary isn't subject to the 10% early-withdrawal penalty with this method, and the assets in the account can continue to grow tax-free for the next five years. Like the other methods, another beneficiary can be selected for this inherited account.

Lump-Sum Distribution

This is a pretty direct method to select, and it is usually chosen if the beneficiary needs or wants the money the soonest. When selecting this option, there is not going to be an account that remains open for asset-growth. The beneficiary will receive all of the funds in a lump-sum, and there will only be taxes on these contributions if the account was less than five years old when the original account holder passed away.

Since this is a fairly straightforward method, there is little else that the beneficiary can learn when selecting it. While the bank where the original account holder opened the Roth IRA might be able to provide a little advice, they won't be able to say much because the money now essentially belongs to the beneficiary. They are free to do whatever they want with it—spend it, save it, donate it, or put it into other bank accounts. This method definitely provides the most freedom with the funds, but it essentially provides the least benefits because there is no more room for these assets to grow.

Understandably, some spouses may not want to choose this option but have to in order to keep up with the expenses of their lifestyle. Going from a two-person household to just a sole-earner is a difficult transition to make unexpectedly. The beneficiary might need this money to pay for funeral expenses or other expenses that arise upon the death of the original account holder. This is definitely not a greedy choice for a beneficiary to make, even if it seems like they just want the money as quickly as possible. Since they inherited the money, they are free to do what they wish with it, and you never know what they might be struggling with financially at the moment that the original account holder dies. Unfortunately, many expenses tend to arise after death.

Non-Spousal Inheritance

When you inherit a Roth IRA account as a beneficiary and you are not the spouse of the original account holder, you also have options as to what you can do with these funds. There are three that you can choose from.

- Open an Inherited IRA, Life Expectancy Method
- Open an Inherited IRA, Five-Year Method
- Lump-Sum Distribution

By taking a look at these options, you'll see that you can do exactly the same things as you can if you were a spouse, minus the spousal transfer method. Each of these options that are provided to a non-spousal beneficiary follow the exact same rules and regulations as the ones that were detailed above. Basically, it all comes down to how soon the beneficiary wants to have access to the funds and if they wish to grow the assets that are already in the account. You can either set up your own Roth IRA account, which will continue to grow into an even bigger nest egg, or you can take the lump-sum distribution option to have access to the money right away.

This is a very personal decision for the beneficiary to make, and it all depends on what is going on in their lives at the time of death of the original account holder. If the beneficiary is still young, it is probably wise to select options one or two because they can continue to grow their wealth with this inheritance. It is a financially sound decision to make, but everyone has their own reasons behind their decisions. You never know when you might need access to emergency funds or how much debt you might have to pay at the time that you receive this inheritance. As long as the Roth IRA account was set up correctly, the beneficiary should have no issues making a selection and then doing what they need to do with their inheritance.

No Beneficiary or Wrong Beneficiary

You may be wondering why not having a beneficiary can lead to a negative outcome. While this isn't a guarantee, it definitely complicates matters if you pass away and do not designate a beneficiary to inherit your funds. Several things could happen if you do not select one or if you pick the wrong one. This section will highlight exactly why the choice is an important one to make and why you should give it some serious thought, even before you open a Roth IRA account.

If you die and do not have a beneficiary selected, then your money will essentially be placed into your estate. This may not be a problem if you have a will in place, but if you also do not have a will, then the state gets to decide what to do with your assets. Depending on where you live, different laws may apply. In some states, if this ends up being the case, your assets are divided up between your spouse and your children, if you have them. There are two potential problems that could arise by leaving it up to the state—you won't get to decide how the money is divided and your loved ones won't get to experience the same tax benefits that they would have if you had named them as beneficiaries.

This means that, while your loved ones might end up with portions of your inheritance, they can be heavily taxed for it depending on what the state laws say. Also, the five-year rule will most definitely apply once they inherit your assets. This is why opening your account as early as possible is important. Not only does it make your life easier but it also sets your loved ones up for an easier future, as well. Handling a death is a very difficult matter to process, but also having to handle financial allocations can add a lot of stress and become a burden to your loved ones who are simultaneously trying to grieve. When you select a beneficiary, or beneficiaries, from the start, you are trying to make things as seamless as possible. Think about your loved ones and the future. While nobody likes to dwell on the idea that they will pass away, it is a realistic and important aspect of life to consider when there are assets to be left behind.

Keeping up with who the current beneficiary is will also become an important part of having a Roth IRA account. Imagine that you got married young and you named your spouse as your beneficiary. Then, you got divorced and remarried later in life. If you never changed the beneficiary on your Roth IRA account, this will not be updated automatically to reflect your current spouse. You need to make the active decision to change this distinction. If you passed away before changing this, then your first spouse would end up with this inheritance instead of your current spouse and children. It just creates a messy and potentially upsetting situation if you don't pay close attention to who your beneficiary is.

No matter what happens or what options your loved ones pick, they're likely going to feel overwhelmed because of the nature of the decisions they'll have to make. It's recommended that they speak with your financial advisor, if you have one, or hire one of their own to help them with this inheritance that has just fallen into their laps. Making big decisions like these can be very difficult when you have just lost someone that you love and care about so much, and that is part of what a financial advisor is there to help you with—they understand that these instances occur, and they can help your loved ones make the best financial decisions going forward.

The Positives

When you list a beneficiary on your Roth IRA account and you do it the right way, your loved one(s) experience many positive benefits. Not only is life made easier for them, but you also get to feel good about what happens to the money that you've been working so hard to grow in your life thus far. When a beneficiary is listed, they are given the chance to either continue growing this money as you had been doing, or they can withdraw it as needed. Either way, someone you love and trust will now be in charge of your funds after you are gone.

Listing a beneficiary gives you both peace of mind because the money won't go to your estate and potentially get lost under any particular state laws. Without a beneficiary, your loved ones might feel like they know exactly what they want to do with your Roth IRA funds, yet they won't have any legal power to do so unless they are your beneficiary or unless it is explicitly mentioned in your will. Even so, with a will and no Roth IRA beneficiary, you are at risk of having the money added into your estate and being taken over by state laws. It's better to be safe than sorry, and it's so easy to write in a name, even if you feel that your beneficiary might change over time.

Life happens quickly, and most people will have to change their Roth IRA beneficiary once, even twice in their lifetime. The great thing is that no matter what, you always have the ability to change who this person is. Just mention it to your financial advisor or log onto your account to see if you can change your beneficiary online. There are no waiting periods or rules that you must follow for changing the beneficiary. Life can happen in the most unexpected ways, but that doesn't mean you need to provide your bank with a detailed reason as to why you're changing your beneficiary. All you need to do is make the request that you'd like to—the decision is entirely personal.

With a beneficiary in place, this gives your loved ones one less thing to worry about after you pass away. They are already going to experience many overwhelming burdens that require decision-making, and on top of this all, they are going to be grieving. Regardless of who your beneficiary is, making this selection during your life is going to alleviate a lot of the pain that your entire family feels after you pass away. It tells the bank exactly what your intentions are, and then they simply have to follow through with these wishes. Since there isn't more than that, your family won't have to try to get together and discuss what should happen next.

Some family dynamics aren't healthy to begin with, and you never know what might happen in several year's time. You can't guarantee that everyone is going to get along, and death naturally brings out many difficult and negative emotions to process. It's probably going to be hard for your family to all sit down together to decide what should happen with your Roth IRA funds. There will be a million other things running through their minds, and this decision is made a lot more difficult if there are some people that don't get along.

Once your beneficiary has your Roth IRA account in their possession, they do have some choices to make, but these choices are surrounded by financial freedom. We've discussed the options that spouses and non-spouses can take with these accounts in the case that they do become the receiving beneficiary. While nobody wants this to happen or thinks about the moment it might, you can feel at ease knowing that your loved one(s) still have choices when it comes to what they think is best for the money or if they need to withdraw it and begin using it to ease the expenses that have arisen. If you have a Roth IRA account right now with no beneficiary listed, it's highly recommended that you select someone based on all of the information discussed. It's not too late to add them to your account.

Mistakes to Avoid

Complied by professionals, there are four mistakes that should be avoided when it comes to the handling of Roth IRA accounts and their estates. These are the most common and learning about them now will allow you to avoid following in their footsteps. Not only are these mistakes burdens to deal with later in life, but they can come with costly consequences.

Failing to Name a Beneficiary

As you know, this is one of the most common mistakes made. People fail to name a beneficiary, mostly when they first open their account because they don't see it as an important step. You might feel that you don't have anyone in your life who is that close to you, but you still need to select someone in case anything does go wrong. Life is not a guarantee and leaving your account unclaimed is only going to complicate things. Whoever does happen to be closest to you at your time of death is going to have to deal with the bank, with lots of negotiations, and with lots of decisions that they would've avoided had you selected a beneficiary. Roth IRAs encourage you to think about your future, and choosing a beneficiary is no exception to this plan.

Choosing the Wrong Beneficiary

The term "wrong" beneficiary might sound intrusive, but it promises some good advice. Typically, spouses will list one another as beneficiaries if they both have Roth IRA accounts. This isn't necessarily a bad strategy, but if you have kids together, then you might want to consider one of you leaving the Roth IRA to the younger generation. Imagine that you both pass away. Since you were the only ones listed on each other's accounts as beneficiaries, your children will eventually have to go through the same burdens of figuring out what to do with the money and how to divide it evenly. This is something that can cause a big rift in even the strongest of families. Your life expectancy isn't a guarantee, but if you do have children, consider naming them instead of your spouse.

Establishing a Trust Incorrectly

There are some cases where a Roth IRA account is rolled over into a trust after the original account owner passes away. This can be a good idea, as long as you've selected the proper trust. Also, the issue of making sure you name beneficiaries comes into play. This is a plan that you can make with your financial advisor when you are still living. If you'd rather place your Roth IRA account into a trust, that's up to you, but you must make sure that you do it correctly so your loved ones get what they are intended to get. To correctly do this, you need to place the Roth IRA into what is known as a conduit trust. This is the kind that does take out RMDs (Required Minimum Distributions) each year, and your family will have to keep up with that, so bear that in mind.

Not taking out Required Minimum Distributions

Regardless of if a trust is involved or not, many beneficiaries might not realize that they do need to start taking RMDs within the year of your passing, by December 31st. This rule applies to non-spousal beneficiaries. While you never had to take out any RMDs during the time that you owned the Roth IRA, it might be a good idea to explain to your non-spousal beneficiary that they are going to have to do this. If they fail to do so, they are either going to be made to withdraw all of the funds at once. This can ruin things for them by making them pay more taxes because they are now in a higher tax bracket, or they can be subject to substantial tax penalties for not following the rules.

If you can avoid making these mistakes, then your family should have no problems knowing what to do with your Roth IRA account after you pass away. With a very clear distinction of who gets what, the next steps are up to them and protected by the rules that come with the account.

10

INVESTMENT MINDSET

In this final chapter, you are going to learn how to get into an investment mindset when it comes to the way you manage your money. Before owning a Roth IRA account, this is something you typically didn't think about. With any regular checking and savings accounts, there is no tie-in with investing and getting into that headspace. You know that if you want to see the most monetary growth during your lifetime, you need to become comfortable with investing your money. This chapter is going to give you all of the tips, advice, and tricks that you need to know to stay on top of your investment strategies.

Getting into this mindset can feel foreign, especially if you've never been there before. It's something new that you'll learn along the way, though. Having a Roth IRA account can bring out the best in you—it allows you to think both logically and creatively to come up with different strategies that you can use to grow your nest egg. Be aware that what goes up can also come down. If you aren't careful, fear and greed can get in the way of your investment strategy. If you succumb to these feelings, you might end up making careless mistakes with your money that you'll regret.

To make sure you are handling everything that deals with investing correctly, you need to get into that investment mindset and stay there. It is a strong mindset to have, and it does require some quick-thinking at times. You'll be able to master this mindset for yourself, confidently making decisions for your money that will allow it to grow and work for you. Ultimately, the goal is to be able to switch on auto-pilot mode as your investments double, even triple. You'll be able to do this with the right knowledge and the right investment mindset combined. By creating a strategy that makes you feel both confident and comfortable, you are going to see a lot of wealth and success in your future.

Common Hurdles

There tend to be three common hurdles that you'll face when you first start investing money. The reason that they are considered common is that a lot of people experience them, especially when they are first starting out with investing. If you feel that you can identify with these hurdles, you don't have to worry or panic—the point of acknowledging that you feel this way is to eventually reframe your way of thinking and to correct the behaviors. You can do this! It isn't too hard or over your head. You've already learned so much about Roth IRA accounts and retirement accounts in general. Investing is just the second part of this puzzle that you will master.

Emotional Investing

Believe it or not, your personal emotions can cause you to make poor decisions while investing. You might feel that you want to invest in certain stocks or funds solely because they are companies that you love and know or maybe you are trying to follow another investment plan that you know someone else is already following. No matter the case, you should consider that investing is not entirely a personal matter. While it's a very personal decision as to where you invest your money, try not to get emotionally involved in the process.

The Solution

Having a financial advisor to guide you is going to be the ultimate solution to this problem because they will provide you with a third-party objective view of how you should manage your money and investment choices. Since they won't be emotionally involved in the decision-making process and it's ultimately up to you in the end, they'll be able to best advise you on what you should do.

Thinking about the mantra "buy low and sell high" is another piece of advice that will help you to keep your emotions far from your investment choices. It simply means that you should buy stocks when they are at their market lows and only sell them when the market is high. In prior chapters, this strategy has been discussed. If you buy a stock while it's at a high, this can seem like a promising investment, but you are essentially paying the most money for the stock during this time. The same can be said for selling low—if you want to sell your stock while the market is low, you may end up losing out on the financial gain that you deserve. This can even impact the original amount you invested, causing you to actually end up with less money than you originally put in.

It can be very hard to let go of stocks that you can see are peaking. In any other situation in life, this can seem counterproductive, but the investment world is different. This is exactly when you need to sell them if you plan on moving your money around. The more that you do this, the more you'll realize that this is an effective strategy that has been working for decades, and you aren't the only one who is first learning how to use it.

Lack of Knowledge

Having a lack of knowledge on any subject is automatically going to put you at a disadvantage. Whether you think that the information is over your head or not important enough to investigate in detail, this can hurt your chances of effectively growing your wealth in the way that you want. Everyone wants to see their investments doing well, but you already know that stock markets fluctuate daily, almost guaranteed. You need to breathe through these fluctuations, remembering that they are never going to be the permanent resting place of the market. Through consumer needs, the economy, and other factors, you'll definitely see the market change before your eyes countless times as you begin investing—this is normal.

The Solution

By reading this book, you are already placing yourself one step ahead of the game. Through the knowledge you have already gained, you are educating yourself on how to invest properly. If you ever need to look back on any of the topics discussed for reference and guidance, this is exactly what the book is for. To better understand a topic, you need to do your own fair share of research on it on your own, even if you do have a financial advisor on your side to assist you. When you have this knowledge, you'll have a better understanding of your advisor's suggestions, putting you at an even greater advantage in knowing how to handle your investments.

Try not to look at the ever-changing market on a daily basis. If you do, you definitely don't need to obsessively watch as the numbers climb and plummet. The stock market can be unpredictable at times, and if you become fixated on the numbers, this is going to be sure to stress you out and potentially lead you to make rash decisions that aren't going to fare well for you or your investments in the end.

The best strategy to follow is to become completely educated on the topic of investments, always researching something when you don't fully understand it. You can also ask your advisor any questions that come up because that's what they are there for. Try not to make this the biggest part of your life or else it will be sure to burden you in the future. With a clear head and all of the correct information, you'll be able to avoid this mistake fairly easily.

Myopic View

What this means is that you've lost sight of the bigger picture. Investing is a very action-packed process at the moment that it's happening. You have to decide where to put your money, how to put it there, and how long you plan on keeping it there. All of this is very present-oriented decision-making, but you still need to widen your lens—think about the future. Imagine your investment in a year from now, five years from now, and even all the way up until you envision yourself retiring. When you only look at what is currently happening, you aren't planning for your future—you're only planning for what may or may not happen tomorrow.

There are few other decisions that you have to make in life that fluctuate quite as much as investing does. The market is going to change frequently, and you must accept the things that you can't change or control. However, what you can control is what steps you decide to take next. By keeping an eye on the market at a reasonable level, you should be able to determine if making a move is even necessary in the first place. There are times when you might be better off staying put for a while. Never forget about the bigger picture.

The Solution

Redefine the term "future." When you think about your future, you need to think about it as mentioned above. The future is not only tomorrow. It is when you reach your next milestone in life, it is a few years from now, and it can even be decades from now. When you keep this in mind, it'll prevent you from only seeing things as they are unfolding currently. Your financial advisor will also be sure to bring this up to you, reminding you that things can change when you least expect them to. This is what investing is all about.

To maintain a true investment mindset, you need to become more open and willing to face the fact that you are essentially taking a risk when you invest, but that is where risk tolerance comes in. To review, this is your personal level of comfort regarding how much you're willing to invest and how you're willing to do it. Also, know that your risk tolerance can change over time. With experience both due to age and familiarity with the market, your risk tolerance is bound to evolve, much like any other skills that you learn in life.

How to Stay Motivated

Investing money takes motivation, probably more than you currently think you have. While you have to stay motivated at your job, with your family and friends, and through every other area of your life, this leaves little room to spend any additional energy on your finances. The thing about being motivated to invest is that it doesn't take up 100% of your time or attention. Just a little bit of care can lead to a lot of growth. These tips will remind you of how to do this and which strategies to take.

Learn to Monitor Performances

The main way to stay motivated is to simply stay in touch with what's going on in the market. You don't have to check it daily, or even every other day. Make it a part of your schedule to check on the market once a week. This is something you can probably commit to without adding an extreme amount of stress to your life. As you do this, you'll understand it more because you'll be reading more about it.

Take a look at the ups and downs because there will be plenty. If you have money currently invested in certain markets, of course, you'll want to pay close attention to those trends. You already know that there isn't a need to panic if you see a dip in the market because this doesn't indicate that it's time to sell. Just keep monitoring how your money is doing.

Identify Weak Behavioral Patterns

You may need to look inward to see why you are lacking motivation. We all want to eat healthier and work out more, but this takes motivation, too. If you have these weak behavioral patterns in your life already, you are most likely going to apply them to the way you handle your money, too. Identifying them is the very first step because this brings you awareness of their presence. From this point, you can then take a look at what your options are.

Making a change is never easy, but think about how much easier your life will become after you make this change. Think about how this can affect the way you care about and manage your money. While money definitely doesn't buy happiness, it can make you feel secure and comforted knowing that you are prepared for your future. Use this to promote healthy change in your life.

Stay Committed to Necessary Changes

Once you figure out what needs to be changed and how to change it, then you need to hold yourself accountable for keeping up with this change. To do this, you might need to rely on a loved one or someone that you trust to remind you to stay on track—most people do. This is nothing to feel ashamed of. Life gets busy, and you can easily become forgetful by falling into the same habits of your past.

To truly stay on top of your changes, you must remind yourself daily of why you are making them and how they will eventually benefit you. Using a rewards-based system will keep you willing to go through with these changes. For example, if you give up going out with your friends once per week to put that money into your Roth IRA account to invest, think about the fact that this money can double while it's in there. This is twice the money that you had before while only having to give up one recreational event.

Gear Up to Deal with Losses

One of the best ways to deal with a downward trend in a market that is relevant to you is to set your ego aside. While it may feel bruised, you need to accept that these losses are going to happen, and they'll happen more than once. Being a great investor has a lot to do with maturity. As you invest more and become more familiar with the market losses you'll endure, you'll also gain a newfound sense of financial maturity.

These losses might make you feel personally attacked at the moment, but understand that the markets don't know who you are. They aren't aiming to make you lose out on a great investment opportunity. It helps to remind yourself that everyone else who invested in a market that's declining is also hurting right now, too. You aren't alone, and you know how fast that scenario can turn around. A once-losing market can turn into a winning market overnight.

Gather Experience in your Investment Strategy

You'll probably learn about countless investment strategies when you first begin investing, but it's smarter to stick to one strategy and become as much of an expert as you can. When you are placing your energy into too many strategies at once, this is how you will become quickly drained of the motivation to do anything. Put the energy that you do have into this one strategy, reading up on it during your free time and committing your extra energy to it when you feel that you have some to spare.

Of course, have a backup strategy in mind, just in case. Your primary focus should be your main investment strategy, though. This strategy could come about through research you've done on your own or it could be a recommendation from a professional. No matter where it originated, do your best to fully understand it and to learn all about it. Realize that strategies can evolve much as the markets can, so it's important to stay on top of them.

Learn to Accept Other Possibilities

When you can accept that your current strategy isn't working, this doesn't mean that it's time to sell immediately. What this means is that a big brainstorming period is about to begin. You need to look into the realistic possibilities of what you can do next and what would be the best option for you to take. Whether you are doing this alone or with help, it's important to participate in this part of your investment strategy because these are the critical thinking skills necessary to keep your money growing for years, even decades, to come.

You should always be weighing your risk vs. reward, otherwise known as your risk tolerance. How comfortable are you with losing and how much are you willing to put in? Investing is like a big gamble, and another individual's personal preference can be entirely different from your own. This is okay. What matters most is that you feel comfortable because this is your money and your future.

Adopt an Objective Approach

As you are staying motivated to invest and watching the markets, try to remain as objective as you can. This means that you shouldn't uphold any expectations as you watch the markets rise and fall. Try not to "predict" too much in the beginning since you still have so much to learn. When you're able to take an objective approach, this is going to kickstart your critical thinking. Your ego will start to back off once it realizes that it plays no role in this part.

As mentioned earlier, the market crashing has nothing to do with you personally. When you are an investor, you are only another gear in the larger robot that continues to move. While your importance shouldn't be questioned, you definitely have to put your role into perspective while you're investing—don't take anything too personally!

These are only a few tactics that you can rely on to stay motivated while you invest. As you use these tips to your advantage, you might even be able to develop some of your own that work out even better. Remember that you have more power than you think you do and the more knowledge you are willing to obtain, the more secure you will feel about what's going on with your money and investments.

Managing Greed

When money is involved, there is a feeling that can rise to the surface known as greed. While you may not be a greedy person yourself, it's still possible to feel greed when it comes to what happens to your money—this is natural because nobody wants to lose. Everyone wants to invest in great markets that triple their profits and set them up for life! You aren't the only one with this goal, but you can't let your own greed get in the way of your success. As you try to navigate the world of investing, you must also keep your greed at bay. Here are some tips that will help you do this.

The Solution

An important thing to remember is that greed is based directly on fear. You feel greedy because something is threatening you. This might be the potential downward spiral of a market you have invested in, or maybe you feel fearful that other investors are doing better than you and making more money. To keep your greed in control, you need to acknowledge and manage your fears. They are natural to have in life, especially when it comes to trading and investing. This is an unfamiliar topic for you, so it'll naturally bring up some unknown elements.

Instead of letting these unknowns scare you, think of them as exciting opportunities. You never know how they may end up working out in your favor, and you can always make them known by taking the time to understand them instead of staring at them fearfully from the corner. Nobody likes to admit when they are scared, but this isn't anything to feel ashamed of. You'll get through this, and you'll learn a lot along the way.

Have a Plan

No matter how much money you are going to invest, you need to have a plan. This plan is going to be the blueprint that you can follow as you are guided through this journey. When you have a plan, there is little room for greed to come into the picture because you already have your own objective. Since you know what your end goal is and what you want to see with that end goal, you can focus on this instead of the greed that tries to enter your life.

Make sure that you put all of your spare energy into your plan instead of into any greed that surfaces. When you commit your energy to positive things, you are going to manifest positive results. Unfortunately, the same can be said with negativity. The more negative elements you focus on, such as greed, the more negative manifestations you'll end up with in your life.

Lower Trading Sizes

If you can tell that you are becoming greedy and you don't like the way it feels, there is a quick remedy—lower your trading sizes. This simply means that you can lower the amount of money you are trading, just for right now. By doing this, you'll be able to get your greed under control and remind yourself that this isn't a competition—this is your life and what you are doing to secure a great nest egg for your future and potentially the future of your loved ones.

This step only needs to be temporary, until you are able to get back on your feet and feel confident about trading once again. When you feel the greed subsiding, then you can slowly begin to invest more money into the market. Much like gambling, investing can also become pretty addicting. If you see markets operating positively, you'll naturally want in on this action. Soon enough, you'll be investing larger and larger amounts of money. Know that larger isn't always smarter. You need to remember your plan and stick to it because it was tailored with your lifestyle in mind.

Keep a Trading Journal

You might be wondering how journaling will help your greed at all in this situation—it can actually make a huge difference! Not only will your journal remind you of what has been going on in your markets of interest, but you'll also be able to see in your own words what has been happening with your money. You can include your personal feelings about each trade that you make, and this can guide you in the future as you attempt to make more of them.

By taking a look at the bigger picture, which would be a full trading journal, this is a great way to come up with a new strategy for your investments if you ever reach this point. You'll be able to see exactly what works and what didn't work to make your best-educated decision on what to do next. Plus, venting out your frustrations in your trading journal can be really helpful if you are experiencing losses. Writing things down instead of keeping them in your mind will prevent these feelings from turning into greed or fear.

Learn from Others

Even if you don't have other investors in your life, you can still read about success stories online. Do your part by researching those who've had great success in trading and investing. You can take notes on their strategies and what they ultimately ended up doing to reach the point of success that they've reached today. This may even inspire you to alter your trading plan a little.

It will also humble you to read about their failures and losses—everyone has them, even the most successful investors. A pattern you'll probably notice is the lack of greed that leads to success. Those who are able to put their greed aside are more open to success in life, and this is how you need to think, as well. Try to remind yourself that greed is an energy vampire, and it will drain you if you allow it.

Take Some Time Away

Sometimes, you just need to walk away from the computer screen. A very small step such as walking away from the market, even if only for a moment, will help you manage your greed because it prevents you from getting to the point where you start feeling upset. There is always such a thing as too much, even too much success. No matter how well or how poorly your investments are doing, there comes a point where you need to just walk away and focus on other things.

You have so many other responsibilities and recreational activities in your life that you can focus on instead of trading. If this isn't your full-time job, then it doesn't deserve your full-time attention. Remind yourself that your greed can start to impact your personal relationships with other people. If you have a lot of greed in your heart, this will manifest into a bad mood. By having this mood constantly, you might be upsetting your spouse, children, friends, and other loved ones without even realizing it.

If you ever feel yourself approaching any level of greed that makes you uncomfortable, you now have these tips to follow that will help bring you back down to a humble state of being. We all need these reminders from time-to-time, and you are no exception. Make sure that you are feeling good about your investment strategy, and you won't experience a lot of the greed that tries to come up.

Conclusion

Through the time you spent reading this book, you've learned a lot about retirement. Now you know what a Roth IRA account is, how much you can contribute to it, and what the rules are regarding withdrawing your money. Most people use Roth IRA accounts as self-led retirement accounts. Given the financial freedom that you have, a Roth IRA account allows you to invest your money into any stocks, bonds, mutual funds, indexes, or CDs. Plus, since the money that you contribute is after-tax money, you don't have to worry about paying any taxes while withdrawing your funds. While there are no rules on when you can withdraw your contributions, there are some that surround the earnings you make on them.

You learned about the five-year rule, meaning that the contribution must stay in the account for at least five years with the earnings in tow if you want to be able to withdraw the earnings penalty-free. This is the main rule that you need to remember, but otherwise, having a Roth IRA account doesn't come with many others. If you need help with investing your funds, that's what a financial advisor is for. They'll let you know about the market and what they believe smart investments would be for your goals. You can also invest without the help of an advisor, but it's recommended that you use one in the beginning as you are still learning.

Another reason why someone might want to open a Roth IRA account is to use it for emergency savings. A Roth IRA differs from a liquid savings account because of its earning capabilities. Since you are investing your money into the market, it has the potential to grow and to create a lot of wealth. In any other savings account, you only rely on an interest rate to carry you forward, which usually doesn't amount to much. Another option that people use Roth IRA accounts is for early retirement. If you know that you're going to retire early or if you'd eventually like to, they serve as great nest eggs.

Overall, you now have all the tools necessary to go out and open your own account. When it comes to your portfolio management, you have the choice to either make it a very hands-on experience or allow an advisor to manage your assets for you. There are also varying degrees of choices in between. With a Roth IRA account, there's little to worry about because your money is safe. You know where it is at all times, and you know where it'll go once you pass away, as long as you correctly choose a beneficiary.

With these tools that you've learned, you should have all of the financial confidence to get out there and start preparing for your future. It's never too early, and it's also never too late. No matter your age, what you do for a living, or where you're at financially, opening a Roth IRA account is going to provide you with additional wealth that you didn't have before. Not only this, but the money can grow exponentially! Since the rate of growth is so quick, you have the possibility of doubling, tripling, or even quadrupling your investment. These exciting possibilities only add to the intrigue of opening a Roth IRA account and having a real plan for your future.

About the Author

Daniel Hardt is an investor, entrepreneur, and ex-financial advisor based in the heart of San Francisco. He served his community as a financial advisor for 15 great years and used his knowledge of finances to retire at the young age of 39. As an early retiree, this advisor-turned-author now invests in spending more time with beautiful wife and two children.

Passionate about financial independence, Daniel grieves over the American school system's failure to properly equip the next generation with financial independence, which is why he hopes to reach a larger audience with his books.

When he's not trying to change the world, he can be found on a jog with his dog Theo in Golden Gate Park or talking about his plans to convert his van into a camper and drive cross country with his family.

Acknowledgement

Thank you to my parents, for raising me to be who I am today.
To my wife who supports me unconditionally.
To my children who keep me young.
To my team for helping realize my dream for this book.

Thanks for reading! Please add a short review on Amazon and let me know what you thought!

Thank you and good luck!
Daniel Hardt

References

Appleby, D. (2020, October 30). IRA Contributions: Eligibility and Deadlines. Investopedia.
https://www.investopedia.com/articles/retirement/05/021505.asp.

Chen, J. (2020, August 29). Index Fund. Investopedia.
https://www.investopedia.com/terms/i/indexfund.asp.

Chen, J. (2020, September 16). How Rebalancing Works. Investopedia.
https://www.investopedia.com/terms/r/rebalancing.asp.

Chorpenning, A. (2019, November 22). What Is an Average Roth IRA Return? SmartAsset. https://smartasset.com/retirement/average-roth-ira-return.

Coombes, A. (2020, November 17). Mega Backdoor Roths: How They Work. NerdWallet. https://www.nerdwallet.com/article/investing/mega-backdoor-roths-work.

Coombes, A. (2020, November 20). The Pros and Cons of a Roth IRA. NerdWallet. https://www.nerdwallet.com/article/investing/roth-ira-pros-and-cons.

Cussen, M. (2020, December 14). Avoid These 4 Roth IRA Mistakes in Estate Planning. Investopedia. https://www.investopedia.com/articles/financial-advisor/110916/4-mistakes-clients-make-roth-iras-and-their-estate.asp.

Folger, J. (2020, December 14). Roth IRA Beneficiary Rules. Investopedia.
https://www.investopedia.com/roth-ira-beneficiary-rules-4770500.

Fontinelle, A. (2020, August 28). When Can You Lose the Rights Over Your 401(k)? Investopedia. https://www.investopedia.com/retirement/401k-know-your-rights/.

Friedberg, B. (2020, November 22). Traditional and Roth IRAs: Benefits and Drawbacks. Investopedia.
https://www.investopedia.com/articles/financial-advisors/120815/iras-advantages-disadvantages-and-which-one-right-you.asp.

Greenberg, D. (2020, September 22). What happens if I go over my IRA contribution limit? Merrill Edge.

https://www.merrilledge.com/ask/retirement/excess-roth-traditional-ira-contributions.

Hogan, C. (2020, October 21). What Are Mutual Funds? daveramsey.com. https://www.daveramsey.com/blog/what-are-mutual-funds.

Kagan, J. (2020, August 28). What Is a Financial Advisor? Investopedia. https://www.investopedia.com/terms/f/financial-advisor.asp.

Kagan, J. (2020, November 7). Roth IRA Conversion. Investopedia. https://www.investopedia.com/terms/i/iraconversion.asp.

Lake, R. (2020, November 4). Can I Contribute to an IRA If I'm Married Filing Separately? Investopedia. https://www.investopedia.com/married-filing-separately-ira-4772024

MacBride, E. (2020, November 16). Backdoor Roth IRA. Investopedia. https://www.investopedia.com/terms/b/backdoor-roth-ira.asp.

MacBride, E. (2015, October 14). Jack Bogle: Follow these 4 investing rules-ignore the rest. CNBC. https://www.cnbc.com/2015/10/14/jack-bogle-follow-these-4-investing-rules-ignore-the-rest.html.

Mercadante, K. (2019, April 4). The Pros And Cons Of A Roth IRA Conversion. Money Under 30. https://www.moneyunder30.com/pros-and-cons-of-a-roth-ira-conversion.

Ngo, S. (2015, March 22). The Pros and Cons of a Roth 401(k). CheatSheet. https://www.cheatsheet.com/money-career/the-pros-and-cons-of-a-roth-401k.html/.

O'Shea, A. (2020, October 23). How to Do a Roth IRA Conversion, and How to Time It Right. NerdWallet. https://www.nerdwallet.com/article/investing/roth-ira-conversion.

O'Shea, B. (2020, December 14). Budgeting 101: How to Budget Money. NerdWallet. https://www.nerdwallet.com/article/finance/how-to-budget.

Probasco, J. (2020, December 17). Worth the Wait: The Roth IRA 5-Year Rule. Investopedia. https://www.investopedia.com/ask/answers/05/waitingperiodroth.asp.

Rodgers, R. (2020, August 12). Roth IRAs and The Pro-Rata Rule. Rodgers & Associates. https://rodgers-associates.com/blog/pro-rata-rule/.

Roth Conversion Ladder. Mad Fientist. https://www.madfientist.com/wp-content/uploads/2016/07/roth-conversion-ladder.png.

Roth conversions. Vanguard. https://investor.vanguard.com/ira/roth-conversion.

Segal, T. (2020, September 29). Target-Date Fund. Investopedia.
        https://www.investopedia.com/terms/t/target-date_fund.asp.

Segal, T. (2020, November 13). The Complete Guide to the Roth IRA.
        Investopedia. https://www.investopedia.com/terms/r/rothira.asp.

Singh, R. (2013, August 27). 3 Serious Investment Hurdles and how to overcome
        them? Holistic investment planners, financial planning Chennai, Private
        wealth management Chennai.
        https://www.holisticinvestment.in/investment-hurdles/.

Smith, T. (2020, September 16). Manage My Own Investments? Are You
        Kidding? Investopedia.
        https://www.investopedia.com/articles/stocks/08/invest-on-your-own.asp.

Strange, J. (2020, February 21). Pros & Cons of Traditional vs Roth 401(k).
        Investopedia. https://www.goodlifefinancialnova.com/blog/pros-cons-of-
        traditional-vs-roth-401k-1.

Snow, R. (2019, April 5). How to Manage Fear and Greed in Trading. DailyFX.
        https://www.dailyfx.com/education/trading-discipline/managing-fear-
        and-greed-in-trading.html.

Travillian, A. (2020, August 28). Hot or Not: Single Stocks in Your Portfolio.
        Investopedia.
        https://www.investopedia.com/articles/investing/072915/single-stocks-
        your-portfolio-pros-and-cons.asp.